OLD SILVER

FOR MODERN SETTINGS

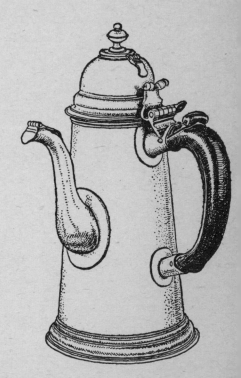

OLD SILVER

FOR MODERN SETTINGS

Edward Wenham
Illustrated by Edgar Holloway

Spring Books · London

Originally published 1950
This edition published 1964 by
SPRING BOOKS
Westbook House . Fulham Broadway
London

*Printed in England by
Richard Clay and Company Ltd
Bungay, Suffolk*

PREFACE

KNOWLEDGE IS FOSTERED by curiosity, and in gratifying our curiosity concerning man's cultural development it becomes clear that this development is indicated in the things which man contrived to satisfy his wants; and the things themselves acquaint us with his ingenuity in adapting natural forms from which later and more advanced people evolved the many graceful shapes that reached their perfection during the eighteenth century.

To-day, there are few who are not interested, to a greater or lesser extent, in the furnishings which bygone generations used in their homes. That interest is considerably increased when supplemented by some knowledge of the origin and evolution of the various household articles which came into use through the centuries and of which many are in use to the present day. This applies particularly to domestic silver, which, as time went on, came to be represented by a wide variety of articles of different designs and which has always had a certain intimate association with those who owned and used it.

Numerous questions have been met with regarding the origins of the shapes (and the names) of familiar silver objects and these, with other rather neglected aspects, have been kept in mind in writing the following pages. This book is therefore largely the story of eighteenth-century domestic silver which is still obtainable and still useful in a modern home, rather than an academic descriptive treatise of rare and historical specimens.

While, however, this has been the primary purpose, chapters have been included describing the silverwork of the later Tudor period and the seventeenth century; and these chapters also touch on the various observances associated with the standing-salt, standing-cup and other ceremonial silver vessels; observances, too, which, in modified form, have survived to the present day.

In view of their importance and the general lack of familiarity with them, the hall-marks of England, Scotland and Ireland are described in detail, yet in a manner which will make them easily understood when identifying any punched on a piece of silver.

Those chapters are accompanied by one or more illustrations of the principal mark or marks referred to in the text. In addition to those used at different periods by the London and English provincial, Edinburgh and Dublin assay offices, marks adopted by various English, Scottish and Irish towns are also described and illustrated.

Most of us prefer to get our experience at first hand rather than through the medium of another; but if advice may not always be accepted, it will, if sound, remain as a steadying influence to rely upon in case of need. For that reason, the chapter based upon past personal errors and oversights is offered as a sheet-anchor to steady any venturesome craft. Again, the suggestions as to early silver that can find a useful place in a modern home are the outcome of experiment and observation over some years.

Care has been taken throughout to avoid excursions into the fields of technicalities and the descriptions relating to the evolution of the various shapes and the ornamental forms are in every-day language; moreover, each of the chapters dealing with the different articles is accompanied by illustrations showing the characteristics of the several styles which were fashionable during the eighteenth and early nineteenth centuries.

My grateful acknowledgements are due to Messrs. Christie, Manson and Woods, Ltd., and to Messrs. Sotheby & Co. for many of the photographs from which the drawings were made.

Equally, am I grateful to my friends of the British Antique Dealers' Association, who, at all times, generously allow me to have photographs, and for other favours I am privileged to enjoy at their hands; and in connection with this book, I would mention Messrs. William Bruford & Sons, Ltd., Crichton Bros., The Goldsmiths and Silversmiths Co. Ltd., Harman & Co. Ltd., H. R. Jessop, Ltd., Thomas Lumley Ltd., S. J. Phillips and Walter H. Willson, Ltd.

Also I would express my thanks to Messrs. William Comyns & Sons, Ltd., for the several illustrations of the modern copies which are referred to in Chapter 26.

E. W.

CONTENTS

THE LINE ILLUSTRATIONS

THE PHOTOGRAPHS

These photographs appear between pages 84 and 85.

SECTION 1
How to Read Hall-marks

CHAPTER ONE

LONDON MARKS

TO-DAY, THE TERM 'hall-mark' commonly denotes personal reliability and efficiency or that some article is of fine workmanship, as in a recent advertisement which in large type claimed the commodity offered was the 'hall-mark of value'. And so generally has it come to be accepted and used in this sense that its original meaning is probably unfamiliar except to those who are interested in silverwork. Actually, it might be written 'guild-mark' as it derived from the ancient craft-guilds organized in the Middle Ages which were the ancestors of what are now known as Livery Companies.

As far back as seven hundred years ago the different crafts or industries began to form themselves into united bodies or guilds—the word comes from the Anglo-Saxon *gild*, meaning a company supported by subscriptions. And it was these guilds which instituted the system of apprenticing and which regulated the training of craftsmen. As soon as an apprentice had served his time he was allowed to work as a journeyman; after he had saved enough money to start a shop of his own, he deposited a piece of his work—his masterpiece—for approval by the guild and this being accepted, he paid his fee and was recorded as a master-craftsman.

In time, these groups of craftsmen were established in all the larger centres in England, and, during the reign of Edward III (1327–77), each guild adopted a distinctive dress or livery, and so came to be called Livery Companies, by which name they are known to the present time. The word 'guild' was changed to 'crafts and mysteries' ('mystery' meaning trade or occupation);

the former Alderman (head-man) being replaced by a master and wardens and each guild had its own meeting place or guild's hall.

There is mention of a Goldsmiths' Guild in 1180 and, about a century later, it had become so powerful and important it was given authority to examine all gold and silver articles at the guild's hall and to stamp those which were satisfactory with a mark—hence the expression 'hall-mark'. The first established mark was the now familiar leopard's head which—except during the High Standard period 1697–1720—has been used by the London Goldsmiths' Company since 1300.

In that year, it was ordered that all silver should be of 'esterling allay' (sterling alloy), or, as it is called, sterling standard. An early writer suggests that the word 'sterling' derived from the Germans who were termed Easterlings by the English, from their living Eastward, and who were called in by King John to reduce the silver to its due fineness and such silver money in ancient writings is called 'easterlings', later abbreviated to 'sterling'.

Pure silver is too soft for silverwork and a proportion of copper is added to harden the metal, the proportion allowed being controlled by law. This explains the purpose of the various assay offices to which the makers submit all articles of gold or silver for testing as to their 'due fineness' and marking with the several punches before they can be offered for sale.

It is not unusual for even fairly experienced collectors to regard the tables of silver marks with a certain trepidation. Admittedly, these curious symbols and their accompanying date letters are somewhat unintelligible at first sight, but, after some study, they begin to 'make sense' and their meaning becomes clear. And it is not long before the interpretation of the various combinations offers a fascinating hobby, when each punch is read in conjunction with the other marks on any piece of silver. Moreover, they show the master-goldsmiths of bygone days evolved a simple yet safe method of protecting the public from fraud and a means of catching any member of their craft who disobeyed the regulations. For any such misdemeanours, they inflicted uncomfortable punishments, such as the loss of an ear or two, and counterfeiting or transposing marks was punishable by death.

All the various marks found on London and other British and Irish silver were adopted solely to ensure the silversmiths used a proper standard of metal and not, as we moderns are apt to assume, to assist us to determine the date and makers. Each separate mark has a particular significance and while, as we shall see, variations occur in certain marks, these variations were usually adopted for a specific purpose. Thus, in London, there are six basic marks, two of which were changed in the later period and which in order of appearance are:

1. The leopard's head crowned
2. The maker's mark
3. The annual letter
4. The lion's passant guardant (full faced)
5. The lion's head erased
6. The figure of Britannia

1722–3: John Edwards   1728–9: Edward Cornock

First year of New Standard (1697): William Keatt

First year of Queen Anne (1702–3): Thomas Ash

Examples of Hall-Marks and Makers' Marks

The later changes were the removal of the crown from the leopard's head and the lion to profile instead of full faced. The sovereign's head was an additional, temporary duty mark.

THE LEOPARD'S HEAD

When Edward III appointed the Goldsmiths' Guild to decide on the quality of gold and silver and to 'certify' a piece with the mark of their guild's hall, the mark we know as the leopard's head was adopted; this is really the head of a lion looking directly at you. Here, we need not concern ourselves with the many types of leopard's head which appeared before 1600. It might be possible to assume that each die-cutter of early times expressed his own temperament in his interpretation of the leopard's face —which being so, they seem to have been a happy lot of men during the late Tudor time, for all the leopard's faces after about 1550 have the cheery countenance of a well-fed bucolic who 'likes his sup of good beer'.

Starting with the cycle, 1598–1617, the leopard's head has a thin serious face with large ears and some trace of whiskers in a punch which follows the outline of the head.   In 1618 (the commencement of a new cycle), the face is slightly broader and the whiskers more noticeable and this more cheerful face continued with certain minor variations until 1680 when the punch, instead of following the outline, became an irregular rounded shape.   This punch continued in use until 1697 when the High Standard silver was introduced and the leopard's head replaced by the lion's head erased (cut off at the neck with a jagged edge).

With the restoration of the old standard of silver in 1719–20 the leopard's head was again used, though it would seem the Assay Master of the Goldsmiths' Company met with some difficulty in finding a head that pleased him.   During the following sixteen years no less than six different punches were cut and used.   For the first two years it was a smaller clean-shaven face in a shield with a pointed base; the next eight years, a bewhiskered bucolic; then a return to the smaller face but this time with whiskers.   Two years later it rather resembles a gargoyle and three years after that, it is again clean-shaven and in a shield with a pointed base, but noticeably smaller, and while the pointed shield is retained, the face is changed again seven years later (1736).

In 1739 the head assumes the cat-like 'whiskers' found with all the leopard's head punches from that year to the present time. In 1756, the face is wider and the punch is a straight-sided shield with straight top and rounded base; and while from 1776 to 1820 there are minor variations in the animal's face, the shape of the punch retains the straight sides with rounded base, but the corners of the top are clipped.

From 1821–2, the leopard's head was shorn of its crown and from that time it has varied in appearance from that of a starved

1598–9 to 1696–7

1719–20 to 1739

1739–40 to 1820–1

from 1821–2
Examples of Leopards' Heads

alley cat to one of those pampered and well-fed felines, at no time having any resemblance to the regal animal it is supposed to represent.

Many details have been mentioned in the foregoing remarks, such as the shapes of the punches and variations in the leopard's head. These might seem unimportant, but where marks are worn and more or less illegible, the minor differences are of considerable assistance in determining the date at which a piece was assayed.

THE MAKER'S MARK

Every student of British and Irish silver acknowledges the immense debt we owe to the late Sir Charles J. Jackson who devoted some twenty years to assembling the valuable information contained in his *English Goldsmiths and their Marks*. This work includes some thousands of marks used by different assay offices and British and Irish silversmiths from as far back as the latter part of the fifteenth century.

Sixty-three years after the adoption of the leopard's head as the

London guild mark, it was ordered that every master-goldsmith should have a 'mark or sign' by which he could be identified and that it should be punched on all work submitted for assay. In those early days the mass of the people knew little of letters, which explains why shops, like modern inns, were identified by a hanging sign instead of a street number and silversmiths marked their work with some symbol. It is rare indeed to find letters used as a maker's mark until the beginning of the seventeenth century but, unfortunately, it is not possible to identify more than a few of these or the various signs such as a bull's head, a pelican, a pair of bellows, a key, a negro's head and a small host of others.

As time went on, the symbols were gradually replaced by letters which were doubtless the initials of the silversmiths and, by the middle of the seventeenth century, the signs had almost disappeared except where they were used with the letters in the same punch. In fact, symbols are found frequently with initials until the middle of the following century, after which they are rare.

That the Goldsmiths' Company recorded the names against the marks of those who were admitted as master-goldsmiths is shown by an account of the London Assay Office in *The Touchstone* printed in 1677 which says:

In this office is likewise kept for publique view a table or tables artificially made of columns of parchment or velom, and several of the same sorts; in the lead are struck or entered the workers' marks (which are generally the first letters of the Christian and Sir-names) and right against them . . . are writ and entered the owners' names.

These records, however, have never come to light, but the copper plates in which impressions of makers' marks were made from 1675 to 1697 are still preserved at Goldsmiths' Hall, although there are no records of the names. Since 1697, ink impressions of makers' marks have been made in the books of the Company and the name and address of the goldsmith recorded against each mark.

When the High Standard or Britannia silver was made compulsory in 1697, the silversmith's 'mark or sign' was changed from the initials of the christian and surnames to the first two letters of the surname. This form was used exclusively until the old standard of silver was restored in 1720 when, for nineteen years, silversmiths used two punches—the first two letters of the surname on work of the higher standard or Britannia silver and the initials of the christian and surnames on the lower or, what is commonly known as, the sterling standard.

This practice evidently caused some trouble to the Assay Office for, in 1739, the silversmiths were ordered to destroy all the marks that they had on hand and register new punches of their initials which were to be in letters of an entirely different character from any they had used previously. The effect of this is evident in the large number of makers' marks in script and old-English letters appearing in the lists for some years after 1739.

THE DATE OR ANNUAL LETTER

Since they were first established, the assay offices in Britain and Dublin have worked in cycles, each year being identified by a single letter and each cycle by a different type of alphabet. The London office has a twenty year cycle and uses all the letters of the alphabet from A to U except J, the U being replaced by V in a few of the earlier cycles, the last instance being for the year 1735–6. This letter is referred to as the assayer's or warden's mark, the alphabetical mark, the year letter or, as we more commonly speak of it to-day, the date letter.

One cycle—1678–9 to 1697—is one year short of the twenty owing to the change in the standard of silver and a consequent change of alphabet in March, 1697. Each letter therefore, while in use for only twelve months, actually covers a part of two years, which explains the reference to two years when writing the date of a piece of silver.

Many, when they first become interested in silver marks, experience some difficulty because date letters of the same type are repeated in different cycles. Obviously, there are not enough distinctive styles of alphabets or founts, as they are called in the

1660-1   1758-9

1838-9

world of printing, to 'ring the changes' indefinitely. This repetition need cause no confusion,. however, if the letters are read in conjunction with the several variations occurring in the other marks used during the various cycles.

Example being more instructive than explanation, we illustrate the hall-marks of three different years in which the old English capital ℭ is used, namely 1660-1, 1758-9 and 1838-9. Actually there are slight differences in the letters, but these when punched in the metal are not seen readily. In any event, there is no need to rely upon these minor variations, for when the date letter is read with the accompanying marks, any doubt is removed.

Thus: For the year 1660-1, the old English ℭ is accompanied by the broad-faced bewhiskered leopard's head crowned and the lion looking at you full face, both in punches following the outline. It therefore indicates a date before 1680, after which the punches were no longer cut to the shape of the leopard's head and the lion. And as this type of alphabet was used for the first time for the cycle 1658-9 to 1677-8 and is the third letter, it represents the year 1660-1.

At first sight, the same three marks occur for the year 1758-9, but, when studied, the following differences are noticeable: The letter is in a shield with a double cyma (⌣) curve base and the top corners are clipped; the leopard's head is still crowned but the full beard is replaced by cat-like 'side-whiskers' and it is in a straight-sided shield with a rounded base. The lion has also changed from the rather cramped outline to an oblong punch with the double cyma base and clipped or rounded top corners.

No long study is needed for the third example, the duty mark (the head of Queen Victoria) alone dating it as after 1837. And when the leopard's head and the lion are compared with those of the two earlier years in which the old English 𝕮 is the date letter, two very marked differences are noticeable: The leopard is without the crown and the lion is in profile instead of full faced, both of which changes were made in 1821–2.

THE LION PASSANT

1598–9 to 1820–1

after 1820–1

Examples of Lion Passant

Although this mark is more commonly referred to as lion passant, it was, in the strict heraldic sense, passant guardant or looking full faced until 1820–1 and passant (in profile) after that year. This difference is of material importance in instances where the accompanying marks are damaged or more or less illegible. There seems to be no official record as to when this mark was first used, but Jackson advances strong evidence that it was adopted in 1544–5.

It has been suggested that its introduction was the result of the lowering of the quality of the silver coins, and that it was adopted by the London Goldsmiths' Company as an indication that any silverware marked with the lion was of sterling standard and not made from metal obtained from melting the poor quality silver coinage. This punch appears on all silver assayed and marked at the London Assay Office for the past four hundred years, except during the period when the high standard silver was enforced (1697 to 1719–20), such variations as occur in the form being in the shape of the punch and the change in 1821–2 from the lion full faced to profile, described above.

LION'S HEAD ERASED AND BRITANNIA

from 1697 to 1718–19

These marks were the outcome of the extravagant use of silver during the reign of Charles II. The demand became so immoderate that the silversmiths resorted to melting the current coinage to obtain metal and eventually it was impossible to obtain sufficient silver to supply the Mint.

After various efforts to encourage owners to send their silver to the Mint had failed, an Act was passed by which the standard of metal for silver articles was raised from 11 oz. 2 dwt. to 11 oz. 10 dwt. of pure silver to the pound (12 oz.) troy. In plainer language, the amount of alloy for domestic silver was considerably decreased, but that for the coinage remained as it had been previously. This meant that when an article was taken to the Assay Office for marking it had to be of metal of the higher standard, otherwise it was confiscated and the maker punished—and in those days the penalties were severe.

Another change which resulted from the raising of the standard of metal occurred with the hall-marks: The former leopard's head and lion passant were replaced by the figure of Britannia and a lion's head erased. These marks were used exclusively during the last five years of William III, the whole of Queen Anne's reign and the first five years of George I.

For some reason, many people are under the impression that these two marks were impressed only on silver made in the early eighteenth century; in fact it is quite usual to hear it spoken of as 'Queen Anne'. But it is well to remember that although the old standard of metal and with it the familiar leopard's head and lion passant were restored in 1720, the high standard metal continued to be and still is used. And any articles made of the high standard of metal are marked by the Assay Office with the figure of Britannia and the lion's head erased.

THE SOVEREIGN'S HEAD

1784–5 *1785–6*	*1786–7 to 1819–20*	*1820–1* *to* *1830–1*	*1831–2* *to* *1836–7*	*1837–8* *to* *1889–90*

It could be said that this mark perpetuates the tax-gathering proclivities of George III. It first appeared in 1784–5 to indicate the payment of duty on articles of gold and silver and continued to be used until 1889–90, when the duty was repealed.

For the first two years (1784–5 and 1785–6) the head is incused or impressed in the metal instead of being in cameo or relief as it always was afterwards. Another peculiarity in the mark for those two years is that the head of George III faces left (as you see it) whereas his later heads and those of George IV and William IV face to the right, but that of Queen Victoria faces to the left.

CHAPTER TWO

ENGLISH PROVINCIAL MARKS

MUCH OF THE ancient history of English silver remains in the work made by men far removed from London. And in dealing with the various, often isolated, groups of provincial craftsmen, it is necessary to divide them into two categories: (a) those working in larger centres in which there was a legally appointed or official office where silver was assayed and certified with authorized marks; and (b) those in smaller towns in which the craft was more or less directed by a local guild.

In 1696–7, when the Act was passed changing the standard of silver, the provincial assay offices were deprived of their privileges and were compelled to send the silverwork made by local craftsmen to London. As the only means of transport was by coach, this meant a very considerable delay and expense, in addition to the risk of loss at the hands of the 'knights of the road'. But, as always with unfair regulations, it was not long before means were found to circumvent the edict, and, within five years, assay offices were re-established at York, Chester, Exeter, Bristol, Norwich, and Newcastle. In this way, those parts of England more distant from London were divided into four regions, respectively, north-west, south-west, east and north, each with a legally established authority. All these early offices have ceased to function with the exception of Chester which, with the late-comers, Birmingham and Sheffield, remains active to the present day. Though appointed, Bristol does not seem to have had an assay office.

Smaller centres adopted a town mark by which the work of the locality may be identified. Some marks ascribed to different towns have yet to be verified definitely and these have afforded and still afford pleasurable mental exercise to the enthusiastic votary.

BIRMINGHAM

Dating no earlier than 1773, neither the Birmingham Assay Office nor its marks offer the same historical interest as those of the earlier cities and boroughs. The town mark adopted by the Birmingham Company after its incorporation was an anchor, which has remained unchanged to the present time; the other marks being the lion passant to indicate the sterling standard, the date letter, the maker's mark, and, from 1784–5 to 1889–90, the sovereign's head or duty mark.

CHESTER

In contrast to Birmingham, its now larger neighbour, the story of goldsmithing in the ancient city of Chester can be traced at least as far back as the thirteenth century. Chester was in earlier times a separate principality governed by the Earls of Chester. Consequently, unlike those of other provincial cities and boroughs, the assay office was controlled by the Earl instead of by the English Parliament. From such records as are available, it does not seem that either a town-mark or a date-letter was used by the Chester office until after the short-lived charter was granted by James II in 1685—short-lived because the powers under that charter ceased about ten years later when the high standard silver was introduced.

Chester silver dating before 1686 often bears the maker's mark only, although some is punched STER LING or Sterl; in addition to the maker's mark. After that year, however, the Chester Gold-smiths' Company adopted as a tcwn mark the now familiar three garbs or wheat-sheaves with a sword erect. In some instances, this is accompanied by the plume of three feathers which is the badge of the Prince of Wales who is also the Earl of Chester; occasionally the plume punch is replaced by a sword erect with a riband, or a piece will be marked with the STER LING punch and the town mark omitted.

When, after being suspended, the Chester office was re-established in 1700–1, a new town mark was adopted—the three lions of England impaling the three wheat-sheaves of the Earl of Chester—in plain language, the front half of the three lions on one side of the punch and on the other, a complete wheat-sheaf above and half a sheaf below. A cycle of date letters was instituted and, until 1718–19, these two marks are accompanied by the lion's head erased and the figure of Britannia marks.

In 1719–20, when the old or sterling standard silver was again allowed, the last two mentioned marks were replaced by the lion passant and leopard's head crowned. Sixty years later (1779–80) the earlier town mark of three wheat-sheaves with the sword was revived and this mark has remained in use ever since; one other punch found on Chester silver is the sovereign's head from 1784–5 to 1889–90. The leopard's head, which is uncrowned after 1823–4, was discontinued by the Chester office in 1838–9.

Summarised and including the maker's mark, the punches found on silver assayed at Chester after 1701–2 are:

<blockquote>
Five until 1783–4
Six from 1784–5 to 1838–9
Five from 1839–40 to 1889–90
and   Four since 1890–1
</blockquote>

EXETER

There are no records of an official assay office operating before 1701–2 in this once important centre of goldsmithing, though it is known that a goldsmiths' guild was active there in early Tudor times if not before. This guild adopted the town mark of a Roman capital x, usually with a crown above in a circular punch, a mark which has been found on a large number of examples made by different Exeter silversmiths during the sixteenth and seventeenth centuries; some few others dating after about 1680 are punched XON or EXON, the abbreviated form of Exeter.

Upon the establishment of an authorised assay office in 1701–2, Exeter was directed to use the city arms—a triple towered castle

—as the town mark, the earlier x mark being discontinued. Until 1720–1, this mark was accompanied by the high standard punches (lion's head erased and Britannia), the variable date letter and maker's mark.   From 1721–2, the familiar leopard's head and lion passant replaced the high standard marks until 1777–8 when the leopard's head was discontinued.

In 1784–5, the sovereign's head was added and this remained in use until the office was finally closed in 1883.   Therefore, during the time Exeter had an official assay office (1701–1883) silverwork marked these bears: Five marks until 1777–8; four, from 1778–9 to 1783–4; and five from 1784–5 until the office ceased to function.

HULL

Although one of the towns allowed to have its own 'touch' in 1432, the Hull goldsmiths were apparently controlled by a guild. The earliest town mark is a capital H, doubtless the initial of the name, but in the seventeenth century this was changed to three coronets one above the other.   The latest of the relatively few examples known to have been made here date from the early eighteenth century, after which time the Hull silverworking craft finally ceased.

NEWCASTLE

There were goldsmiths working in Newcastle as far back as 1248 and possibly earlier, but there is no mention of a Company until 1536.   The town mark during the earlier part of the seventeenth century is a single castle, but in about 1675–80 it was replaced by three castles—two above one—in a plain shield and this remained unchanged, except for variations in the shape of the punch, until the office was closed in 1884.

Like other provincial assay offices which were re-established at the beginning of the eighteenth century, Newcastle used the lion's head erased and the figure of Britannia until 1720-1, the other marks being a variable date letter and the maker's mark; the lion passant and the leopard's head crowned replacing the Britannia standard marks in 1721-2. An interesting peculiarity occurs with the lion passant mark which shows the animal facing to the right—as you look at the punch—until 1727-8 after which it faces to the left; some examples for the year 1722-3 also face to the left.

Another peculiarity is in the leopard's head which, with the Newcastle marks, retains its crown until 1845-6, whereas in London it was uncrowned twenty-four years earlier. This town did comply with the duty mark, however, and from 1784-5 till the office ceased to function in 1884, the sovereign's head is added to the other five marks, namely: the three castle town mark, lion passant, leopard's head, date letter and maker's mark.

NORWICH

Goldsmiths were working in Norwich during the thirteenth century and an important group of craftsmen were active there during the days of Queen Elizabeth to whom a lengthy petition was presented complaining:

That the Quenes maiesties subjects have ben thereby greatly decyved and abused to the greate defasing and slaundour of so famous and worthy an arte or science. . . . And for that no comon stampp or marke have thereto ben used and occupyed withen the saide cittie whereby the saide works of sylver made and wrought . . . might be stamped and signed.

That petition resulted in the authorized assaying and marking of all silverwork made in Norwich, the first town mark being the lion with a castle above—the city arms—which is found with the maker's mark for some few years after 1565. About 1575-80, the town mark was changed to a rose with a crown above, although the former lion and castle continued to be used, occasionally with the crowned rose.

In 1624, the master and wardens of the Norwich goldsmiths apparently decided they would organize the assay office and run it as it should be run. This ambition was realized for some twenty years, during which time the silverwork was marked with the lion and castle, the rose crowned, a regular date letter and the maker's mark. What happened to the office after that is not recorded, but for the following forty years there is little or no suggestion of any properly authorized marks or of the use of date letters. Among the more prevalent marks found during this 'lapse from grace' are the lion and castle, a crown and a rose on a stalk (uncrowned), each in a separate punch but generally found together.

From 1688 to 1697, when the Norwich and other provincial offices were deprived of their privileges, an effort was made to handle the assaying in a business-like manner, but the decline had gone too far and so, after many centuries, the history of Norwich silversmiths was ended.

SHEFFIELD

Like the other newcomer (Birmingham), the birthplace of the famous Sheffield plate lacks any great interest as a centre of early silverwork. Established in 1773, the town mark then adopted and used since is a crown accompanied in a separate punch by the lion passant—the sterling standard mark—the date letter and maker's mark; and from 1784-5 to 1889-90 the sovereign's head (duty mark).

Before 1824, both the style of alphabets and the order of the letters might be regarded as 'eccentric'. During the first cycle of twenty-six letters (1773-4 to 1798-9) no less than three different types of letters are used and in irregular order; and while the character of the letters of the next cycle is consistent they, too, are in irregular order. A point to observe with Sheffield date letters is, that from the opening of the office until 1843-4, a crown will sometimes be above or at the side of the letter in the same punch.

YORK

Over the years, the first town mark of the ancient city of York has exercised many students and been fruitful of many arguments, some insisting it is half a fleur-de-lis joined to half a leopard's head, while others contend it is half a fleur-de-lis and half a rose. Then two enthusiasts turned up some old records of 1560 and 1606 where it is referred to as 'halfe leopard head and halfe flowre-de-luyce'.

Whether it is half a rose or half a leopard's head is immaterial, as the curious mark, always in a circular punch, cannot be confused with that of any other town or borough—once the York mark has been seen, it is unmistakable, however you care to read the right hand half.   Moreover, York not only adopted a system of date letters in 1559–60, but also used them regularly, and examples of silverwork have been found bearing the date letter of each year from 1607–8 until 1698–9 with very few exceptions.

When the office was re-established in 1700–1, the town mark was changed to a cross bearing five lions, the accompanying marks being the usual date letter and maker's mark, lion's head erased and figure of Britannia, the last two being replaced later by the lion passant and leopard's head crowned.

After being compelled to comply with what is known as the Britannia Standard Act, it might appear that the York silversmiths became indifferent to their former greatness.   Within a few years, their number had diminished to such an extent that the assay office ceased to operate and after 1717, all silverwork made at York was sent to Newcastle to be assayed.

This arrangement continued until about 1780 when the York Assay Office was reopened.   But the day of the York silversmiths had passed and after more than four centuries the office was closed finally in 1858, at which time five marks were used, i.e. the cross with five lions (town mark), lion passant, sovereign's head, date letter and maker's mark.

BARNSTAPLE

This ancient North Devon seaport probably had its own Goldsmiths' Guild in the fourteenth century. Silverwork was made there until the end of the seventeenth century and possibly later, the earliest town mark being a bird in a circular punch. This seems to have been used until 1625 when it was changed to a three-towered castle, at first with the portcullis lowered in the large gateway and later to a single castle with BAR above and UM below—Barum being the abbreviated form of Barnstaple.

Most of the known examples of Barnstaple silver are spoons though both these and larger pieces are among the rarities of early silver.

BRISTOL

There is no mention of an assay office having existed in this famous City, though Bristow, to use its old name, was one of the seven towns allowed 'to have divers touches' in 1443. Some years ago, however, a spoon was found among the silver belonging to Temple Church, Bristol and later a milk-jug came into the hands of Crichton Bros. each of which was marked with five punches—a maker's mark; date letter; lion passant; leopard's head crowned; and a ship sailing from behind a castle. The last mark, being the arms of Bristol, allows the assumption that silver was assayed there and that the City Arms were used as the town mark.

OTHER ENGLISH TOWN MARKS

In the study of what has been called the geography of English provincial silverwork, an appreciable number of different

emblems have been found.   Some few of these have been definitely identified, others, while tentatively ascribed, remain specula-
tive and many more are unascribed.   Where an identification
has been made, it has been based upon the origin of the emblem
forming the mark, as in the case of Plymouth which used a
saltire cross between four castles, the arms of the borough.

This applies also to Shrewsbury—a leopard's head—the arms of
the City being three leopard's heads; Lewes where the town mark
is, in heraldic phraseology, *checky, or. and az.; on a sinister canton
gules a lion rampant or.* (in less esoteric language, a checkered shield
with a lion standing on his hind legs in the top right hand corner)
which is taken from the town seal.   Sandwich adopted half a
lion joined to a ship's hull, from the seal of the Cinque Ports of
which the town is one; King's Lynn, three dragons' heads; Leeds,
the golden fleece from the town arms; Lincoln, a fleur-de-lis;
and Taunton, the capital town of Somerset, used a T and a tun,
or T on tun, a rebus of the name.

King's   Leeds   Lincoln   Taunton
Lynn

CHAPTER THREE

MARKS ON SCOTTISH SILVER

EDINBURGH

WHILE SILVERWORK made in this Scottish city was examined and marked by the deacon of the guild and the maker as early as 1457, it was not until 1485 that Edinburgh adopted a town mark which was the three towered castle from the arms of the burgh; and this same mark, varied in form at different periods, has been used by the Edinburgh Assay Office to the present time. Until 1680, all work assayed there bears this three towered castle, the maker's mark—usually the initials in monogram—and the deacon's mark —also usually in monogram.

No date letters were adopted until 1681 when the Edinburgh Goldsmiths' introduced regulated cycles; so from that year it is possible to ascertain the date a piece was assayed, when the date letter is accompanied by the other marks, namely, the castle, the maker's mark and the initial or initials of the assay master which replaced those of the deacon.

These four punches are found until 1758–9 when, as the record puts it, Edinburgh plate (as silver is referred to) was to have 'the stamp or impression of the Scots thistle in place of the initial letters of the Assay master's name'; and the thistle has remained ever since. Therefore, from 1759–60 (except from 1784–5 to 1889–90 during which time, the sovereign's head was added) Edinburgh marks, while varied in form, have remained basically the same—the castle, the thistle, date letter and maker's initials.

GLASGOW

On June 15, 1639, the citizens of Glasgow heard a 'proclama-
tioun anent Silver Plait. The said day it is ordainit that publica-
tioun be made throw the toun, be sound of drum, that the
inhabitants of this brughe bring their haill [whole] silver plait to
be bestowit in defence of the good commoun cause in hand . . .'
which 'proclamation' explains the scarcity of silver made before
about 1700 and punched with the mark known as the 'tree, fish
and bell'.

This curious combination which is the Glasgow town mark is
an oak tree with a bird on the top, a bell hanging from a branch
and a salmon with a ring in its mouth at the base of the tree (later
across the trunk). It is traditionally supposed to be connected
with a story in the life of St. Kentigern of Glasgow, A.D. 601.
The tree represents one on which the Saint hung a bell to call
his barbaric flock to worship at a religious settlement he had
started on the banks of the river where Glasgow now stands;
but the real romance lies in the fish holding the ring which
symbolizes the help given by Kentigern to a naughty queen.

According to the legend, Queen Cadzow allowed her affections
to stray and fell in love with a handsome soldier to whom she
gave a ring which the king, her husband, had put on her own
finger. Unfortunately, word of this little adventure came to the
king who, by chance catching the soldier asleep, snatched the
ring from the man's finger and threw it in the river. Then he
went back to the royal stronghold and asked the queen for the
ring he had given her.

She sent a messenger to the soldier to bring back the ring. In
despair at hearing it was lost, she sent for St. Kentigern and asked
him to help her. Being a wise Saint and a man withal, he already
knew of the queen's little affair; he was also by way of being a
magician, for he went to the river Clyde and caught the very
salmon that had the ring in its stomach. So the king and queen
lived happily ever after and the queen's love affair and the power
of Kentigern are perpetuated in the salmon and the ring

which are part of the Glasgow arms and the mark punched on silver.

While it has always 'pictured the story', the details of this mark vary at different periods. In most of the earlier punches, the fish is shown at the base of the tree, the bell hanging sometimes on the right and sometimes on the left, occasionally with the letter G at the other side of the tree. After about 1800, the fish is across the trunk and twenty years later the letter G is omitted.

Apparently, no properly authorized assay office was established in Glasgow until 1819 when the Glasgow Goldsmiths' Company was incorporated and the craft legally regulated. From that time, the usual variable date letter has been used and this, with a standard mark—a lion rampant—added to the town mark. It is therefore possible only to determine definitely the date of a piece of Glasgow silver from 1819–20, since when the date letters have been regularly used.

Apart from the addition of the sovereign's head during the period the duty was imposed on silverwork, the marks remain unchanged until 1914–15 when a thistle was added. At the present time, therefore, the marks on Glasgow silver are: (1) The tree, fish and bell—town mark; (2) lion rampant; (3) thistle; (4) date letter; (5) maker's mark.

ABERDEEN

Formerly, there were two Aberdeens—Old and New—each of which had its own guild of Hammermen who are referred to in the old records as far back as the fifteenth century. The earliest town mark was the first two letters of the name, AB which was later changed to ABD. During the early seventeenth century, three castles in separate punches were added sometimes to the letters and, about a hundred years later, whenever they are used the three castles 'are two above one in the same punch. This last mark is not unlike that used by Newcastle, but there is no difficulty in distinguishing the one from the other as the Aberdeen castles are usually with the letters ABD in roman capitals or script, while those of Newcastle are accompanied by various other punches including a date letter, which was not used by Aberdeen.

BANFF

Some ten or twelve goldsmiths are known to have worked in this ancient Scottish seaport, from the late seventeenth to the middle of the nineteenth century though examples of their work are rare. Most of the known examples are spoons which usually bear one of several abbreviated forms of the town name—BANF, BAF, BA, or merely the letter B.

DUNDEE

This royal burgh, described by a sixteenth-century chronicler as 'Dunde . . . quhair mony virtewus and lauborius pepill are in making of claith (cloth)' had its own school of silversmiths until the early part of the last century. The town mark is a pot of growing lilies and while there are variations in the shape, the pot always has two handles. The mark seems to have been used fairly consistently by the silversmiths, occasionally punched twice on the same piece, with a thistle in a separate punch; and there are instances where the pot of lilies is replaced or accompanied by the name DUN DEE.

ELGIN

To seek an example of silverwork made at Elgin is to seek a rarity, for though there are signs that a guild existed there from about 1701 to 1830, the members could not have been very active judging from the scarcity of pieces bearing the town mark, ELG or ELN or the name in full ELGIN. Other more rare marks are the figure of a woman holding a child, used during the first half of the eighteenth century and, after 1790, a punch showing the door of a church is occasionally found with the town name.

GREENOCK

After this Scottish port became a centre of shipbuilding and sugar refining (1760–5) a small group of silversmiths showed promise of developing their craft to some importance. This, however, was not realized and after about 1830 no silverwork seems to have been made there. Several marks indicative of Greenock were used by men who worked there, the principal being an anchor which is by far the most general, a tree (supposed to be a green oak suggesting the name Greenock), and a three masted ship in full sail. Some examples are punched with the anchor only, others with the anchor and tree and others with all three marks.

INVERNESS

Like other Scottish towns, Inverness used an abbreviation of its name, INS which fact was largely instrumental in the identification of the earliest known Inverness silverwork. This piece is a quaich which has been ascribed to about 1640, though the name of the maker MK is unknown, as no official list of silversmiths working in Inverness before about 1740 has so far been found.

In some instances the INS mark is accompanied by a cornucopia or by a curious looking beast intended for a dromedary, and examples are known where an elephant replaces the dromedary, both animals appearing in the arms of the burgh. While a few more important pieces of Inverness silver are known, it is rare that any except spoons become available. The Breadalbane collection which was sold some twelve years ago in Edinburgh included three quaiches and a Highland brooch which bore the Inverness mark, as well as pieces made at other Scottish provincial towns, but such a collection only reaches the public market at long intervals.

PERTH

Formerly the capital of Scotland, Perth is said to have been founded by the Romans more than nineteen centuries ago. It was then known as Victoria, but after the Romans departed, the inhabitants gave it the Celtic name Aber-tha which later became Bertha and thus to the present Perth; and until the seventeenth century it was called both Perth and St. Johnstown, the latter deriving from the fact that the first church was dedicated to St. John the Baptist.

Its ancient emblem was a lamb carrying a banner and this was adopted as the first town mark used by the silversmiths. This has been found on the few known examples attributed to various years from about 1670 to 1710. Later the lamb was replaced by the more familiar imperial, double-headed, eagle which is found on Perth silver down to the early nineteenth century when the bird is sometimes deprived of one head.

OTHER SCOTTISH TOWN MARKS

Of the few other Scottish town marks which do appear, albeit very rarely, we might mention here: Arbroath which used a portcullis from its burgh seal; Canongate, a stag lodged (at rest) and later, a stag's head; Montrose, a five-petalled rose; and Tain and Wick, each of which used the town name in full, TAIN, WICK.

Arbroath   *Canongate*   *Montrose*

CHAPTER FOUR

MARKS USED IN IRELAND

DUBLIN

AS JACKSON REMARKS, the records of the Dublin Goldsmiths' Company are more complete than those of the London, Edinburgh or any other Company. Not only is there a list of goldsmiths dating from the beginning of the thirteenth century, but also one of apprentices for nearly two hundred years and a further list of Quarter Brothers and journeymen. The term Quarter Brother was applied to those who had completed their apprenticeship and to immigrants who were 'allowed to work and enjoy certain privileges by paying quarterly contributions' to the Dublin Goldsmiths' Company.

Dublin had a well-established Goldsmith's Guild at the end of the fifteenth century which was apparently incorporated shortly afterwards, but no regular assay and marking of silverware seem to have been instituted until after 1637 when a charter was granted to the Goldsmiths' Company of Dublin.

Under this charter, the Dublin Assay Office was ordered to use the harp crowned as a standard mark, in addition to which every article assayed was to bear the mark of the maker. A date letter was also adopted and these three marks should appear on any silver marked at Dublin from 1638–9 to 1730–1, the figure of Hibernia being added in the following year. But, let it be said, the chances of finding an example made in that period are to say the least remote for much early silver went to the melting-pot. Moreover, during the early seventeenth century, a very large quantity was turned in to the authorities at five shillings an ounce to be made into coins for what the proclamation called 'the exigencies of state'.

THE HARP CROWNED

It might be said with truth that a harp is a harp; but a study of the many forms used by the Dublin Assay Office over two centuries shows the wide variations that can be introduced to the shape. For the first hundred and fifty years, that is until 1786, the punch follows the outline and during that time there were more than forty variations. In 1787, the punch was altered again, this time to an oval. Seven years later, it was a rectangle with clipped corners and this shape remained in use until 1809. Then it was altered to a heraldic shield, and again—to an oval—in 1821, and during the following twenty-four years it was changed no less than twelve times.

There is a humorous side to this Irish 'mutability', but an acquaintance with the variations in the shape of the harp is of value in determining a date, especially as it was not uncommon for the date letter to be omitted, more particularly during the later eighteenth century.

THE MAKER'S MARK

This follows the same general form as the London maker's marks already dealt with, except that there was no change from the initials of the christian and surname to the first two letters of the surname, such as was enforced in England from 1697 to 1719–20, nor was any change made in the style of mark in 1739.

THE DATE LETTER

Owing to the absence of actual examples of Dublin silverwork for certain years, the late Sir Charles J. Jackson has reproduced only eleven date letters of the first forty years, after the date letter was introduced in 1638–9. From that time, however, his tables illustrate the letter of each year with two exceptions. And here a suggestion: When referring to the letters covering the period from 1679–80 to 1746, it is well to read them in conjunction with the other marks as the styles of the alphabets are similar, and this applies equally to the letters for the years 1747 to 1845.

HIBERNIA

This poetic name is a corruption of the Latin Iverna, the ancient name for Ireland, but the figure of the lady punched on Dublin silver was adopted by the Dublin Goldsmiths' Company not to indicate Irish origin, but to show the payment of a tax of sixpence an ounce imposed by the Irish Parliament in 1730 'to encourage tillage'. And one cannot help seeing a touch of real Irish humour in the idea that silversmithing should assist farming.

Taxes stimulate artifice and dull the conscience and, with the appearance of Hibernia in 1731, forging hall-marks became a popular pastime, perfect dies of the various punches being made and used on silver without reference to the Dublin Assay Office. Then one silversmith named Keating, who was tried for forging the Hibernia mark, claimed successfully it was not a legal punch, but one adopted by the Dublin Goldsmiths' Company without official blessing. That was in 1776, and after Keating won his case, the Revenue authorities suddenly realized the fun and games Irish silversmiths had enjoyed for nearly fifty years. So Hibernia was given an official appointment—not that this stopped the tax dodging, it merely made the dodgers more careful.

If, as is probable, the various changes in the shape of the Hibernia punch were made with a view to detecting the forgeries, the forgers must have been particularly busy from 1821 to 1845 for, during those twenty-five years, the punch was altered no less than twelve times.

Six years after the Union of Great Britain and Ireland, in 1801, England inflicted another 'injustice' by ordering that the mark of the reigning sovereign's head should be used on Irish silver to indicate that the duty had been paid. The Hibernia mark was retained, however, and is still used on silver marked at the Dublin Assay Office—in fact, to-day, its original significance is almost forgotten and it is generally regarded as the Dublin town mark.

It should perhaps be mentioned that the lion's head erased and the figure of Britannia were never used, as the Britannia standard of silver was not enforced in Ireland.

Irish Provincial Marks

Unlike England, where a number of provincial assay offices were established in bygone times, Dublin was the only centre in Ireland with legal authority to assay and mark gold and silver. There were, however, groups of silversmiths in upward of one hundred provincial centres, but as most of their work was sent to Dublin to be assayed, Irish town marks are far fewer than those of England or Scotland. In fact, there are only three that need be mentioned here, namely Cork, Youghal and Galway.

Cork

There is little question that silversmiths were working in this historic city during medieval times, yet there is no record of the craft's activities in Cork until about the middle of the seventeenth century. No assay office was ever established there though the several marks found on Cork silver would indicate that some method was adopted by the Guild for testing the standard of the metal.

During the seventeenth and eighteenth centuries, large quantities of silverwork must have been produced in Cork, judging from the number of names in the lists of craftsmen; and an appreciable amount of silver was obtained from melting Spanish dollars which explains the word DOLLAR punched occasionally on a piece made at Cork.

Most of the known examples dating before the early eighteenth century bear one of the various forms of the town mark which are:

A ship in full sail impressed twice.
A ship between two castles in the same punch, impressed twice.
A ship between two castles each in a separate punch.

Toward the end of the seventeenth century the ship disappeared and the two castles only were used, or in some instances one castle alone—in others the town mark is omitted. The town mark was accompanied by the maker's initials punched twice or three times on the same piece, until about 1720, after which they were generally punched once.

About this time, too, the town mark is discontinued and replaced by the word STERLING which is found as STERLING, STARLING, STIRLING, STER, STERLG, and other abbreviated forms. As a general rule, this mark is in roman capital letters in relief, but it also occurs impressed in the metal.

Unfortunately, no date letters were ever used at Cork, consequently the maker's mark and the style of the article are the only means of assigning the date, for which reason it is always very advisable that the less experienced collector should obtain a reliable opinion when considering a piece ascribed to a Cork silversmith.

OTHER IRISH TOWN MARKS

Youghal, where a few silversmiths worked during the seventeenth and eighteenth centuries, used a yawl as a town mark, though examples are few and far between; and equally rare are any bearing the anchor of Galway. Regarding the latter, it might, at first sight, be confused with the anchor of Greenock, Scotland, but the Galway mark may be distinguished by its being in a punch which follows the outline which is never the case with the Greenock anchor. Limerick, like Cork, adopted various forms and spelling of STERLING.

Youghal   *Galway*

Early Traditions and Some History

CHAPTER FIVE

CUSTOMS OF TUDOR TIMES

EVEN IF SILVER things of Tudor days were plentiful they would have no place in an average modern setting—nor are they what Punch called 'Antiques for the Impecunious'. But they do tell us of the manners and customs of the long ago; and when strolling round any museum such as the Victoria and Albert, it is well worth giving some study to the massive drinking cups, large ceremonial salts and other objects that have come down through the centuries.

Few of the things that we now have in everyday use were known in those early days; but the splendour of the domestic silver shows that eating and drinking in the great houses of Queen Elizabeth's time were accompanied by ceremonial observances which, if perhaps not recognized, have survived in our present-day customs.

One of these observances was associated with the standing-cup and another with the standing-salt. The standing-cups with their covers were upward of 22 inches high and elaborately ornamented with embossed and chased work. In the great dining halls, large numbers of the cups would be displayed on the cup-borde or, as we would know it, sideboard. Most of them were entirely of silver, but others were a coconut or an ostrich egg or a nautilus shell mounted in silver on a tall and often fanciful stem.

These huge cups represent the age-old tradition which might be summed up in 'With whom you share your cup with him share your friendship'. To-day, the raising of glasses to an honoured guest at a formal dinner, that less formal manner 'Here's how' when two or three foregather at their favourite meeting place, and the almost forgotten custom of passing round a quart pot of ale in the taproom of a country tavern, each perpetuates the ancient ceremony of the passing of the standing-cup which is still observed at banquets held in the halls of colleges and City Livery Companies.

Back in early times, a large cup was passed round the company, each in turn drinking to one or two of the others present; the man who drank stood up and held the cup with both hands thus leaving himself open to attack. To protect him from treachery, the man next to him would also stand up to be his pledge. In more modern wording, the second man would be responsible for the safety of the first and he indicated his willingness to pledge the other by raising his sword to defend him while drinking.

One writer in *Curiosities of London* refers to the ceremony at what he terms hall-feasts. After the banquet and grace has been said, the Master and Wardens of the Company drink to their guests. The cup is then passed round the table, each guest drinking from it and wiping the rim with his napkin, before passing it to his neighbour.

This, however, lacks the romance of the more formal practice where the man who pledges another with the cup stands and bows to his neighbour; the latter, also standing, then takes the cover from the cup with his right hand and remains holding it while the other drinks. This symbolizes the old-time precaution of keeping the right or dagger hand occupied and so preventing any treachery toward the one drinking.

There are records of the ceremony being observed at the parish meetings and churchwardens' dinners at St. Margaret's, Westminster. On these occasions, the cover of the cup was held, over the head of the person drinking, by his neighbours on his right and left hand.

There are, too, some quaint customs connected with the ceremony which are peculiar to different localities. An early issue of *Notes and Queries* gives a description of one at corporation dinners in Lichfield. After the first two toasts, 'The King' and 'Weale and Worship', are drunk, then, from a silver cup holding upward of a gallon, 'The Mayor drinks first and, on his rising,

the persons on his right and left also rise.   He then hands the cup
to the person on his right side when the one next to him rises,
the one on the left of the Mayor still standing.   Then the cup is
passed across the table to him when *his* left-hand neighbour rises;
so that there are always three standing at the same time—one next
to the person who drinks and one opposite to him'.

Obviously the great standing-cups were not used when the
gentlemen settled down to their after-dinner drinking party; for
such enjoyable affairs, there were individual silver beakers and
goblets.   And though we no longer use silver drinking vessels on
the dinner table, the shapes of both the beakers and the goblets
are repeated in modern glasses.

Those glasses which we now call tumblers are similar in shape
to the Elizabethan beaker, a shape which was derived from a piece
of an ox horn—the first beakers were a section of horn with the
smaller end closed by a disk of horn.   Again, the modern wide
champagne, port and sherry glasses have all come down from the
silver goblets and wine cups of Tudor times.

After the introduction of hops from Flanders in about 1525,
ale as we now know it became widely popular, and the silversmiths had to produce a vessel of a suitable size which would be
in keeping with the prevailing ideas of splendour.   And so the
tankard made its appearance.

Once again the ox horn was called into service as it had been
for the first beakers.   With the tankards, however, the wider
part of the horn was at the bottom.   An elaborately embossed
silver cover and neck band were fitted to the narrow end and a
rib round the lower part of the section of horn, with a strong
scroll handle fastened to the neck band and to the rib below; the
bottom was mounted with an ornamental foot which was made
to grip the horn.   One of these horn tankards which was made
in 1561 was among the silver from the Swaythling collection sold
at Christie's in 1924.

Horn tankards were fairly small and it was not long before
larger ones of silver or silver gilt replaced them.   Some of the
latter are upward of 8 in. high and of a size more adequate for
the quaffing capacities of the Tudor courtiers.   And while their

ornamental qualities are not repeated, the shape remains in pottery and porcelain jugs of more modern days.

The influence of the ceremonial salt of Tudor times and earlier has survived in the present-day arrangement of the tables at a banquet or formal dinner. The table at which the chairman and the principal guests are seated is still referred to as the high table. This term, 'high table', has come down from quite ancient times and is closely associated with the great standing salt-cellar which was known as the Salt (Fig. 1).

Early books on social etiquette stress the importance of the Salt. For instance, Wynkyn de Worde as far back as 1508 in his *Boke of Keruynge* instructs the steward to 'Set your salt on the ryght side where your soverayne shall sit' and 'at every end of ye table set a salte sellar', thus distinguishing between the Salt and the small trencher salt-cellars.

Until about the middle of the seventeenth century, the master of the house dined with his guests and retainers in the great hall. The master and his principal guests were seated at a table raised on a dais across the end of the hall from which we have the term 'high table', while other tables were at floor level along the sides, which, to all intents, is repeated at a formal dinner to-day.

Another indication of the social status of the various guests was shown by the position of each in relation to the Salt. This symbol of rank was placed on the table in front, but slightly to the right of the master of the house, thus the guest on his right was as near the Salt as the host himself. Other guests were seated on his right or left each according to his social eminence. Others had to be content with the tables at floor level, from which came the old expression 'he sits below the salt' denoting a man of small importance.

So both the seating of the guests according to precedence at a formal function and a hostess placing her guests at an informal dinner perpetuate the former importance of the Salt.

Washing of hands at table was also an important formality in early times and a necessary one because forks were unknown. Each guest brought his own knife, and holding his serving of

FIG. 1. Cylindrical silver-gilt salt. 1585–6. H. 10¼ in.

meat in one hand he cut it into more or less suitably sized pieces which he lifted to his mouth with his fingers.

Obviously, there was need for some hand washing at the end of the dinner. And servants with a ewer, usually holding rose-water, and a large deep dish or basin went from guest to guest and poured rosewater over the hands, catching it in the basin which was held underneath; and then drying the hands with a towel. This age-old custom is another that is among those still observed at banquets held by Livery Companies, though now it is symbolized by each guest merely dipping his napkin into the basin and wiping his mouth. But it survives, too, in our modern finger glasses and in the napkin.

Magnificent services of plates and dishes were made during the reign of Elizabeth though little remains to recall them to-day. One such service with a romantic history came up at Christie's in 1911 when it brought £11,500. It was made between 1581 and 1601 and believed to have been of silver captured from the Spanish Armada. During the Civil War it was buried on Dartmoor to prevent its being seized by Cromwell's men.

In addition to the magnificent silver drinking cups, the quaint medieval wood bowls known as mazers were still used during the Tudor times. These bowls varied considerably in size, ranging from 5 inches to 10 inches in diameter. They were made of what is known as bird's eye maple-wood which has a curious spotted figure and was cut from an abnormal growth in the trunk; hence, the name mazer from the German *masa* (a spot), from which our word 'measles' was also derived.

These plain wood bowls were elaborated with an ornamented silver lip band and, at the bottom of the bowl inside, there was a silver boss or print decorated with some emblem or coat of arms. During the later sixteenth century, the bowls were made deeper, sometimes fitted with a cover and raised on a moulded foot held firmly in place by silver straps connecting it to the lip band. Needless to say, mazers are very rare, but there are several historic examples in the British and the Victoria and Albert Museums; others are owned by different Livery Companies and colleges.

Stoneware jugs, mounted with an ornate silver or silver-gilt neckband and cover and a similar foot, vied with the massive tankards especially during the time of Elizabeth, but they seem to have gone out of fashion toward the end of her reign. These jugs or flagons, as they are sometimes called, have a bulbous body and long cylindrical neck and are from about 8 inches to 10 inches high. Most of them are of German stoneware commonly called 'tiger-ware' from the fact that the mottled surface is somewhat similar to the skin of a tiger.

An appreciable number of the German jugs with English silver mounts are in different collections at the present time and examples not infrequently appear in the auction rooms; others are of earthenware made at Fulham and other English potteries, but these are much rarer. Similarly beautiful mounts were also applied to Rhodian and other Near Eastern ware and to Chinese porcelain which was imported to England during the Tudor period. And tall narrow cylinders of glass or marble were transformed into tankards by the addition of a silver cover, handle and foot. The only marble one that has come to the writer's notice was in the sale of the Swaythling silver in 1924, when it brought £1,350 which is some indication of its rarity.

Spoons of this time were about 6 to 7 inches long with a large bowl and narrow stem which had a figure or other object at the end. During the early Tudor period, the figure of the Virgin Mary was still popular and these are known as maidenhead spoons; others have a bunch of grapes, a sitting lion, a ball or other knop at the end of the stem. The most popular, however, were the seal-top and the more familiar apostle spoons. The former have a circular or, occasionally, a hexagonal disk on a baluster and the latter, which were made both singly and in sets, a figure of an apostle.

A complete set comprises one with a figure of Christ carrying the orb and cross, called the Master spoon, and twelve each with a figure of one of the apostles and the particular emblem with which he is identified. Thus Andrew may be distinguished by a saltire cross; Bartholomew, a knife; James the Greater, a pilgrim's staff; James the Lesser, a fuller's pole; John, a cup and a serpent;

Jude, a halberd; Matthew, a money bag; Mathias, an axe; Paul, a sword; Peter, a key; Philip, a cross on a staff; Simon, a saw; Thomas, a spear. Judas Iscariot was not represented as he was excluded by the Church.

While those quoted were generally used, there are variations, as some of the apostles were associated with more than one emblem.

CHAPTER SIX

PURITAN SIMPLICITY
AND ROYAL SPLENDOUR

BYGONE CRAFTSMEN have recorded in their work, as historians have recorded in words, how radically the way of life was affected by political influences during the seventeenth century. And these influences are reflected with particular clarity in the dissimilar designs of the silverwork which was made during the reigns of the several Stuart monarchs and the Commonwealth.

For some years after James I came to the throne in 1603, the magnificence that had marked the reign of Elizabeth remained fashionable. The standing-cups were of the same imposing size and embossed and chased even more elaborately than those of the preceding period. One style of standing-cup, which appeared in the reign of James I and is peculiar to that time and of which examples still exist, is known as a steeple-cup. It has a conical bowl on a baluster with three ornamental brackets and a tall trumpet-shaped foot. The cover is domical with a small disk at the top on which there are three brackets supporting a high steeple-like finial copied from the contemporary architectural steeple—hence the name steeple-cup.

They were frequently made in sets of three, one slightly taller than the others (Fig. 2), and, although very rare, some of these sets have come down to the present time. One which is hall-marked 1611–12, of which the taller cup is over 19 inches high and the other two 18 inches, appeared at Christie's in 1924 when it was bought by Crichton Bros. for £4,700.

Toward the end of James I's reign it is possible to see the coming of the simpler styles dictated by the Puritans, for while these people had been severely repressed in the reign of Elizabeth their influence is noticeable in the silver designs some years before they rose to power and established Cromwell's totalitarian government, during which time ornamentation or anything that smacked of luxury was taboo.

Large standing-salts continued to be made, some of them with the steeple-like finial but the waning of the importance of the Salt is evident in the use of the simpler bell-shaped type which had been fashionable during the later years of the sixteenth century. These salts which are upward of 11 inches high are actually two bell-shaped salt-cellars, one fitted above the other. The upper one has a domed cover with a large perforated knob so that the two sections with the cover fitted together could be used as a quite imposing ceremonial salt, or, separately, as two salt-cellars and a pepper caster. A fair number of these interesting objects have come down across the years and examples sometimes find their way to the auction room, though to buy one is apt to put some strain on the average purse.

Looking, as it were, down the pages of the craftsmen's records during the time the Puritan influence was dominant, the effects of that dominance shows itself in the plain shorter drinking cups without covers, the severely plain flat-top tankards and the gradual disappearance of the standing-salts. During the later part of the Commonwealth period, the cover with the large salts was discontinued and replaced by three brackets fixed to the rim on which a napkin or dish was placed to protect the salt from dust.

FIG. 2.   Steeple-cup.
1611–12. H. 19¼ in.

The austerity dictated by the Puritan principles affected even the spoons which at this time had an egg-shaped bowl with a flat broad stem and a rectangular stump end. The few silver forks which may have been used as 'eating tools' were rather crude affairs with three prongs and a flat stump-end stem similar to that of the spoons. Both the spoons and the forks of this type are now generally referred to as 'Puritan', although they were apparently introduced from Europe, probably from France, where they are known to have been made some years before they first appeared in England.

After the end of Cromwell's experiment and the return of Charles II, the Royalists, freed from the Puritan control, soon saw to it that all signs of that régime were erased. And to this end they indulged in various forms of extravagant display in which silver was used with unprecedented lavishness. For the first few years of Charles II's reign, there was a shortage of silver, but this was overcome to some extent by following the example of the Dutch and making articles of thin metal and decorating them with large flowers, leaves and fruit in bold relief. This form of embossed work not only gave a light article an appearance of being more massive than it was, but it also strengthened the thin metal.

About ten years after the restoration, however, large quantities of silver were brought to Europe from South America by the Spaniards, and both in France and Spain and slightly later in England, silver was used to an extent unknown before or since in the history of silverwork. Silver was no longer restricted to everyday articles, but was used also for chairs, tables, pedestals, wall sconces, large vases, mirror frames, stools, fire-dogs and even bedsteads, warming pans and bellows.

Few of these extravagant objects have survived other than those which have been preserved at Windsor Castle, Knole and other historic places, though in quite recent years one or two examples including a pair of magnificent fire-dogs (see Fig. 3) have been sold at auction. But there still exist an appreciable number of the beautiful toilet-sets which Charles II and his courtiers would present to their lady friends.

How generous this Merry Monarch was to his various mistresses is evident from the accounts of the furnishings of their apartments. For example, John Evelyn the diarist writing of those which Charles II furnished for Louise Renée de Querouaille, afterwards Duchess of Portsmouth, remarks on the 'tables, stands, chimney furniture, sconces, branches, braseras (braziers), etc. all of massive silver and out of number'; and there is another

FIG. 3. One of a pair of silver fire-dogs. *Circa* 1670. H. 18½ in.

record of a wine cistern weighing no less than 1,000 oz. having been made for the same lady.

Silverwork of this time was not only directly affected by the several political changes, but equally by the improvement in table manners and the passing of earlier usages and customs. The master of the house and his principal guests no longer dined in the common hall with the retainers and servants, but in a separate dining-room. With this change, less importance was attached to the significance of the standing-salt and the standing-cup; the former was superseded by a plain spool-shaped salt-holder about 6 inches high and 9 inches in diameter with four brackets fitted to the wide rim to hold a napkin or a plate as described previously in the case of the larger salts fitted with brackets. And the standing-cup gave place to finely made two-handled cups most of which have a pear-shaped, or to use the more technical term, ogee body.

While this shape was known some years earlier, it was not generally accepted until the second half of the seventeenth century when it became increasingly popular and has remained so since that time. In fact, this same outline was later to be adopted for the splendid tea-pots, coffee-pots, cream-jugs, kettles, casters, and other domestic articles which came into use in the reign of Queen Anne and which are in everyday use at the present time (see Figs. 12, 23 and 37).

Some of the larger two-handled cups with covers were accompanied by a separate salver or stand on a foot (Fig. 4) the purpose of the foot being to allow a servant to hold the salver in one hand when offering the cup. As a contemporary writer suggests, the salvers were 'used in giving Beer or other liquid thing to save the carpit or cloathes from drops'. The salvers of this type were imposing affairs of about 12 inches or more in diameter with a wide boldy embossed decorated rim; one favourite style of decoration was various animals against a background of scrolls and flowers, the cup which had a domical cover and finial being similarly embossed.

In addition to these larger cups which were doubtless for cere-monial occasions, smaller ones of the same shape but without a cover must have been in fairly general use judging from the number which have survived. They are generally referred to as porringers and were probably used as an ordinary domestic vessel for semi-fluid foods, though they are also called caudle-cups and wine-cups. But whatever name may be preferred, they are

FIG. 4. Two-handled cup with tazza or salver.
1664-5. Cup 8 in. high; tazza 15 in. diam.

very desirable little pieces about 2 to 3 inches high with scroll handles and for a favourite child as charming a present as could be desired.

If the size of the tankards is any indication, the consumption of beer during the late Stuart days must have been considerable. They average nearly 8 inches high and 6 inches diameter and are without exception the finest examples of these capacious vessels made at any time. They have a cylindrical tapering body with a flat cover and heavy S-scroll handle and a cast thumb-piece by which the cover was raised and held open by the thumb. Some of them are quite plain, but in keeping with the prevailing desire for ornamentation, others were embossed and chased with a deep band of acanthus leaves round the base or engraved with oriental decoration copied from the imported Chinese procelain.

Some of the tankards have a number of studs or pegs set vertically at equal distances, for which reason they are called 'peg' tankards.   Most of the known examples were made at York and the reason suggested for this is that they were introduced from Denmark, where they were widely popular, to the port of Hull. These fine pieces usually have two distinguishing features in addition to the studs, namely three feet formed as pomegranates and a thumb-piece formed of two of the same fruit, features which the York silversmiths copied from the Danish originals.

Apropos the word 'peg' in connection with the tankards. This came from the expression 'to take one down a peg' which really alludes to the raising or lowering of a ship's colours by pegs—the higher the pegs the greater the honour and *vice versa*.   The late E. Alfred Jones quotes the description of the custom connected with these tankards which was given by Dr. Pegge the seventeenth century antiquary who says: 'They have in the inside a row of eight pins one above the other from top to bottom; the tankards hold two quarts so there will be a gill of ale, i.e. half a pint of Winchester measure between each pin. The first person who drank was to empty the tankard to the first peg or pin; the second was to empty to the next pin, etc. by which the pins were so many measures to the compotators, making them all drink alike the same quantity; and as the position of the pins was such as to contain a large draught of liquor, the company would be very liable by this method to get drunk, especially when, if they drank short of the pin or beyond it, they were obliged to drink again'.

Another curiosity connected with the 'art' of drinking was introduced from Europe, either Germany or Holland.   It was in the form of a woman with a long skirt holding above her head two ornamental brackets between which a small bowl swings on pivots.   In Germany, cups of this kind were used at weddings; the figure was upturned which caused the small bowl to pivot; both the 'skirt' and the small bowl were filled with wine, the bridegroom drinking the contents of the 'skirt' and then, carefully reversing the figure, he presented it to his bride who drank from the small bowl.

Many a wager was laid at drinking parties that the contents of the two wine-cups could not be drunk without spilling any, and one can imagine that as the evening advanced, the likelihood of the drinker winning the wager became increasingly remote. Another amusing wine-cup which came into fashion in the late Stuart days was a small bowl with a rounded bottom which caused it to wobble; these, called tumblers, are dealt with more fully in a later chapter.

Silver forks for use at table with a knife do not seem to have been accepted to any extent until toward the end of the seventeenth century when they had either two (Fig. 6B, 1), three or four prongs. The stems were broad and flat widening to an outline rather like a pear with two clefts or notches cut in the end, from which they get the name trifid, i.e. divided into three. But that the advice contained in some of the earlier books on etiquette that 'each guest should bring his knife' still obtained is apparent from the fact that shark-skin cases containing a fork, a knife and spoon were still made for carrying in the pocket at the end of the century. Both the knife and fork were of steel with silver handles, and though now very rare, examples of these delightful little sets of 'portable table tools' do still exist.

There are various other articles of silver which came into use during the reign of Charles II, and examples in our public museums are worth studying as illustrations of both the extravagant luxury of that time and the effect of foreign influence upon English silver designs.

SECTION 3
Old Silver in Modern Surroundings

CHAPTER SEVEN

SOME RULES TO REMEMBER

CONTEMPLATING THE title of this chapter, the word 'rules' seems to accuse the writer of didacticism. It might have been replaced by 'advice', but that, to use a picturesque Americanism, lacks the same 'punch', so we accept the risk.

In point of fact an interest in old silver, like an interest in gardening, does not rely upon any prescribed rules; rather it gains its stimulation from personal observation and knowledge garnered from enthusiasts who have been longer 'at the game'. And here a warning to beware of the well-intentioned person who bestows upon you that nebulous and foolish compliment 'You have a flair for old silver'. That compliment very often brings humiliation to the 'flairist', because it is apt to lead to his assuming knowledge he does not possess and which can prove expensive to himself and others—as the writer learned in the now somewhat distant past.

There are no short-cuts to the understanding of early silverwork —there would be very little fun in it if there were, for anything that is obvious rarely holds our interest or appreciation. On the other hand, something that calls for scrutiny and study engenders a sense of accomplishment and self-confidence when we have worked out the answer. And the interest grows in proportion to the number of problems we solve. As an American friend once said of the writer, 'Give him a piece of old silver with a worn mark and he'll play for hours.'

With a certain few exceptions, silver articles made in Great Britain and Ireland bear a legal guarantee of quality and proof of the actual year in which they were made, as explained fully in

Section 1 of this book. By the way, unless you have an urge to indulge in a 'Pelmanistic' exercise, refrain from trying to memorize all the many cycles of letters which indicate the dates. Sufficient familiarity with these letters comes in the course of time and even if you have, as you may think, registered them mentally, no memory is infallible and any established silver dealer can supply you with the complete tables in a neat little book you can keep in your pocket.

It has been said that attention is the stuff that memory is made of. And if the attention can be concentrated on concise information, the mind is not cluttered up with unnecessary details and for that reason is more easily equipped with a working knowledge of any subject. Obviously, familiarity with the hall-marks of old silver adds very considerably to the interest, but, broadly speaking, the essential points are far less numerous than might be generally supposed.

The means of recognizing silver made in London after 1697 and the approximate period during which it was made might be summed up as follows: any punched with the figure of Britannia and the lion's head cut off with a ragged edge and one of the curious letters of the so-called 'Court' alphabet dates between 1697 and 1715–16; the next three years are the same Britannia and lion's head but with the roman capital letters A, B, C.

Then there is a longish interval from 1719–20 to 1783–4 during which the leopard's head crowned and the lion passant were used with the letter, but the period is sub-divided by changes in the style of the leopard's head and the shape of the punch of both the leopard's head and the lion; these changes you can become familiar with or you can refer to the little pocket tables.

The next thirty-seven years (1784–5 to 1820–1) are plain sailing because in 1784 the king's head was added to the other marks; nor is there any difficulty in identifying silver made in the following sixteen years (1821–2 to 1836–7) because the leopard's head is without a crown. In 1837 when Queen Victoria came to the throne, her head which is familiar to all of us took the place of the male or king's head and serves to indicate silverwork from 1837–8 to 1889–90 when the sovereign's head was discontinued.

Subject to some few slight variations, the above 'rules' apply equally to silver marked by the assay offices appointed in Birmingham, Chester, Exeter, Newcastle, Sheffield and York. With the exception of Birmingham and Sheffield, each office used the Britannia and lion's head marks during the period these were enforced in London. The ubiquitous lion passant was used by all of them and also, for some years, the leopard's head (crowned or uncrowned) but each added its own particular town mark; the leopard mark was not adopted by Birmingham or Sheffield.

These town marks have been described and illustrated in Section 1, but the term recalls an easy method of becoming familiar with them which was adopted by the writer in the days when his interest in old silver was but a timid bud—a collector who saw it gave it the rather apt name of 'Geography of silver marks'.

Its value is in its simplicity: Trace or draw a fair-sized (about 12 by 8 inches will serve) map of Great Britain and Ireland and mark on it the names of the various cities and towns mentioned in Section 1 of this book. Then if you have the patience and the artistic skill sketch against each the particular town mark or marks by which silver made in the locality can be identified—if, like the writer, you are too unskilled with a drawing-pen, ask a friend to sketch in the marks.

Confidence in your own judgment does not grow in a night and even when that confidence seems to be a sturdy plant, it is well not to rely on it too early. Admittedly, we should learn by our mistakes and we all have to make them, which is why a piece of rubber is fitted to the end of a pencil; but the less 'rubber' we have to use, the stronger our self-reliance becomes.

Some people who admire and would like to own good silver for their homes are curiously diffident of walking round one of the larger shops and asking questions. Yet anyone can gain more real information in those same shops than would be as easily available in the average public museum where every article is 'locked up' and those who might impart any worth while knowledge are generally as equally 'un-get-at-able'.

This writer has been for many years in fairly close touch with the 'professional collectors', as we sometimes call them, both in this country and in America and he has yet to find one who is not willing and eager to explain the distinguishing features of the different periods or, with quiet patience, enlighten the beginner as to the 'mysterious' symbols and hieroglyphics we call hall-marks. Moreover they will extend their helpfulness by illustrating the various points with actual articles of silver from their stock.

Another erroneous but widely accepted idea is that the prices of silver put it beyond the reach of any but the quite wealthy. Admittedly some enormous sums have been paid and they have been well and truly publicized. But it is well to remember that the very fact that they are quoted in the press is itself an indication that they are unusual, if not abnormal.

Impressive bids for silver at auction have been reported in the daily press since 1902 when the Dunn-Gardner collection was sold at Christie's and some of the early specimens brought prices that may be said to have started the upward climb in the curve of values. For example, a Henry VIII small cup on a foot brought £4,100, a James I standing-cup £4,000, and a Henry VII spoon £690. These and other high bids were published as similar ones are to-day; and the average person, not being familiar with the influence of age and rarity, quite naturally comes to regard them as a criterion of values for all silver.

To illustrate this more clearly, we will quote some of the prices paid at that same Dunn-Gardner sale for Queen Anne and Georgian silver which can be taken into every day use: A pair of candlesticks, £28; Twelve silver-gilt coffee spoons, £14 14s.; a silver-gilt kettle and stand, £68; a hot-water jug, £21; a milk jug, £8; a barrel-shaped beer jug, £13; a helmet-shaped cream jug, £4. Obviously these prices would be higher to-day, but they serve to show the very wide difference between those that are brought to public notice and the very much greater number which never appear in the newspapers.

Now a word regarding those who can and are willing to broaden your knowledge and advise you: There are over one hundred and fifty shops handling old silver in Great Britain of which upward of fifty are in London. That one hundred and fifty takes into account only those where the owners are members of the powerful British Antique Dealers' Association and therefore have to fulfil its requirements. Furthermore, they are subject to the rigid regulations imposed by law, the breach of which calls forth some heavy penalties.

Through the many centuries and in our own time, the high quality of silver wares has been enforced to a degree unknown with any other domestic articles. The number of statutory regulations relating to both old and new silver are almost bewildering and all of them are intended to protect the buyer from misrepresentation. By way of some enlightenment as to how careful a dealer has to be, the following are only a few of the many things he has to watch: if an article has been added to or altered in any way he must point this out when he sells it; he may not sell any piece that is not hall-marked; if he happens to sell a hall-marked article which was altered at a later date and the alteration has not been passed by the assay office, he can be fined; if he imports silver ware from a foreign country, he may not offer it for sale until it has been tested by the assay office and marked; if by some unlucky (and unlikely) chance a piece with a forged or transposed hall-mark gets into his shop, he must see that it goes to the authorities, who destroy it, otherwise he is committing a felony which is punishable with up to fourteen years' penal servitude.

It would be possible to continue the list for several pages of this book, but enough has been said to show that in protecting himself against 'inconvenience' the dealer automatically protects you —possibly against yourself. No reputable establishment would take the risk of offering any silver regarding which they had even a remote doubt. All such pieces are sent to the assay office to be vetted and there either commended or condemned.

Particular stress must be put upon your relying upon reputable dealers whether in London or in the provincial centres; and by that is meant those men who have been accepted by and are registered members of the British Antique Dealers' Association or, as it is known, the B.A.D.A.

If, like a young man buying an engagement or wedding ring, you feel somewhat shy of making your first enquiries at one of the larger and more imposing shops, begin by having a chat with the owner of a smaller one. Later, when you have been initiated into the mysteries of silverwork and have been surprised to find that most of the price tickets read far less than you imagined, you will enter one of the larger shops without any trepidation. And there you will find the same spontaneous helpfulness and the same possibility of buying without pauperising yourself—and you will also see objects which you personally may covet, but which your bank account dictates you may not own.

Many silver dealers' shops, both large and small, have a delightful old-world atmosphere. And the unhurried quiet seems to affect those who are perhaps waiting to be attended to, even those visitors to this country whose time is more or less regulated by a 'schedule'.

No man can sell silver with any pleasure unless he has a personal liking for it. Many times a dealer has shown the writer a specimen he has bought but would not offer for sale. In some instances it was because the dealer himself wished to enjoy the pleasure of possessing it, at least for a time; often a particular piece will be 'hidden' until it can be offered to someone who will fully appreciate it.

Apropos 'hiding' for certain customers. Much is to be gained by frankly discussing with the dealer or dealers of your choice, exactly what you are looking for and the approximate price you are willing to pay. That allows him to act, as it were, for you if he sees any likely article at a sale or elsewhere. You need have no fear that because he knows your price limit he will necessarily charge you the full amount; actually his margin of profit will be more in the form of a moderate commission.

That raises another rather interesting point, namely buying at auction. Speaking from a fairly wide experience, the writer's advice is to enjoy the fun of going to the view, select any pieces that appeal to you and then ask a reliable dealer or other experienced person you may know to examine the various articles, and advise you. That advice will include the approximate market value of each piece and if this is within your range, let the dealer buy for you. The probability is that he will be attending the sale in any event and for his services to you he will charge a recognized commission. There is a lot of entertainment at a good auction sale if you are actively interested in a fair number of the lots, otherwise it is very apt to be tiresomely boring.

Incidentally, silver bought at a public sale is warranted in the same way as that bought in a shop, because an auctioneer who sells silver is under the same regulations as a dealer. And this explains why one or more lots are sometimes withdrawn from a catalogue after they have been on view. These withdrawals will serve to illustrate how keen and helpful the dealers are. While silver is on view, these professional buyers examine all the pieces that may interest them and any regarding which they have any doubt they bring to the notice of the auctioneer, who knowing he can rely upon their opinion cancels them from the catalogue.

We have intentionally dealt at some length upon the advisability of depending upon experience in the beginning, because the slower you hasten, the quicker you will arrive at a sound understanding of old silver; and the sounder your understanding the more fascinating it becomes, both as a hobby and as part of those things that bring charm and beauty to a home.

And now a brief dissertation upon what might be entitled 'Slumming for Silver', an often entertaining but, to the unwary, always a risky amusement. Public markets and musty shops in darksome alleys invariably appeal to the sense of romance. If you succumb, see to it that the romantic atmosphere and persuasive tongues do not dull your judgment and sense of proportion. In moments of weakness, it may well happen to any of us, experienced or otherwise, and if you do give way and are caught remember it for what it is—a lesson not to be repeated—and also the old adage *caveat emptor*.

None will deny that the possibility of making a 'find' is tempting, but the keepers behind the heterogeneous mass in the windows of those unkempt 'emporiums' are not there to dispense philanthropy. A bookmaker does not take a punter's money hoping to return it tenfold. So on a 'slumming' expedition be ready to lose your money or at least don't expect to get value for it.

There does come a time, however, when you have 'learned enough answers', that one of these forays may possibly bring some reward. In this we speak from experience because there are among the 'family plate' several highly esteemed articles which were found in unexpected places and obtained at less than their real value. There is a rather charming small fruit dish that when first seen was quite black and lying among some old iron. On another occasion some small three-pronged forks were extracted from a heap of more or less junk on a stall. Admittedly these are early Victorian, but they are the same pattern as those made in the time of Queen Anne, which most people who use them imagine they are.

That is a narration of successes. A more lengthy one might be told of the 'stings' in the days when exercise was being given to the 'flair'—and the experiments of one may and should be of help to others. And the chapter ends with that hope.

CHAPTER EIGHT

OLD SILVER FOR USE AND DECORATION

THINGS THAT PLEASE the eye bring tranquillity to the mind and escape from everyday irritations, for beauty around us gratifies our sense of the complete and the perfect. But this is attained only when that beauty is elusive and springs from those indefinable touches which make a painting great and a house a home—as an ancient aphorism has it, little things give perfection although perfection is not a little thing.

Personal taste and suitability to the surroundings are two important guides in the selection of silver, either for use or ornament. More is naturally required in the dining-room, as it was in the great halls of past ages, but a dining table may glitter like the paste jewellery worn by an actress on the stage or produce an atmosphere of unostentatious well-being. And the latter is always present when the silver is of the plainer Georgian designs upon which Time has laid his softening hand and the table ornaments are in keeping.

Writing this recalls an average sized dining-room to which we were privileged to be invited many times. The table was a double gate-legged type of a size to seat eight comfortably or ten less so. The spoons and forks were the plain Old English pattern except the soup spoons which had the shallow bowls and wavy-end stems; to digress, those soup spoons were found in a market where neither the stall-holder nor anyone else knew what they were, but the present owner liked them and 'took a chance', later discovering they were French, but that was a number of years ago.

The centre ornament on that table was a pierced cake-basket (Fig. 41) holding various flowers, the stems of which were in a shallow oval glass bowl which evidently had been chosen to more or less fit the basket; and the basket was, as it were, centred by four late Georgian columnar candlesticks (Fig. 49). The other silver included four of the small round salt-cellars on legs, and modern reproductions of the little octagonal 'kitchen pepper-pots', sauce-boats, and a large pear-shaped jug (Fig. 27) of the kind used for beer or for filling the punch glasses. The pepper-pots were perfect, but their youth was obvious when compared with the other pieces because, though they were by no means dazzling bright, they lacked the old 'colour'. The dinner service was one of Spode's modern stoneware with a quite simple decoration and years later the writer added a similar service to his household 'crockery'.

Whether to indulge in silver entrée dishes is a matter of choice. But when there are porcelain or stoneware vegetable dishes with the dinner service, the addition of silver ones seems rather redundant. At the same time, a pair of silver entrée dishes are undeniably useful for savouries and various other purposes.

In modern times, the sideboard has taken the place of the former cupborde on which the numerous silver drinking cups were displayed in bygone days. The treatment of the sideboard should be considered in relation to its size and the size of the room. Too much silver on the sideboard is apt to be out of keeping with the character of the room; on the other hand if the sideboard is fairly large, too little may result in a somewhat bare appearance.

Upright objects such as candlesticks, a candelabrum, a tea-urn or an epergne rarely fail to be 'at home' on a sideboard, bearing in mind the size of the top; but it is largely a matter of a series of 'put and take' experiments to arrive at the point where a hostess can walk into the room when it is ready for a small dinner party and feel really pleased with the entire setting.

Of silver as part of the 'tea equipage', it can be said at the outset that with few exceptions the complete services represent varying degrees of the same ugliness. There are some which have one of the straight-sided tea-pots of the late eighteenth century which would grace any tea table, but unfortunately these are few and far between. An opinion may be inspired by personal prejudice or based upon observation. Any expressed here comes from the latter source which would indicate a strong preference for 'building up' a service on the foundation of a globular-shaped (Fig. 8) or straight-sided tea-pot (Fig. 11), the other pieces being added as they become available and the family exchequer permits.

On the other hand, those who own an early porcelain tea-service—and many still do—should be satisfied to add the silver tea-pot only. There is a lot in favour of this arrangement as the tea-pot assumes a certain quiet dignity against the background of the colourful porcelain. Moreover, there is an absence of that awesome formality which one of the early Victorian silver services almost inevitably introduces to the pleasant tea-time hour.

Except for candlesticks, silver articles suitable as ornaments in the strict sense are relatively few. Smaller bowls are useful for short-stemmed flowers on a small table and a larger bowl, of a size in which punch was brewed, is an effective ornament on any table or in an alcove, particularly when it is holding long stemmed flowers supported in the holes of one of the ingenious glass gadgets in the bottom of the bowl.

Though, like the itinerant scriveners of long ago, we now mostly carry our pen and ink, if in the more compact form of a modern fountain pen, an inkstand with one or a pair of the little tapersticks on a writing desk makes an attractive setting, especially if one or two quill pens are put in the holes of the little pot intended for them. Then again, one of the now almost for-gotten bedroom candlesticks and perhaps a pair of snuffers with its little tray adds an old-world charm to a hall table and equally to a dressing table—they seem more natural if a candle which has been lighted is put in the socket.

One effective use of silver we have seen was on the top of a corner cupboard where a large dish or basin was placed against the angle of the wall with a two-handled cup in front. Both these pieces were hand-made copies, the dish which is about 14 inches diameter was copied from one of the quite early rose-water dishes or basins, and the cup which is about 7 inches high from an original made in the time of Charles II. And their soft 'colour' showed that they had been diligently rubbed many times during the years the owner had enjoyed them.

Several articles which are now out of date and are regarded
more as curiosities can be brought back into everyday use even
if not for the purpose they were originally intended.   Marrow
scoops are unusually efficient honey spoons as being narrow you
can 'wind' the honey round the scoop and so prevent its trickling
down; also there is the additional advantage of the length of the
stem.   The writer has assembled six of them and they are still
put to their original use of scooping marrow from bones, which
is a delicacy sadly overlooked in these days.

Argyles which are described in a later chapter may have lost
their appeal as gravy holders, but those with the hot water jacket
are excellent for hot milk or coffee for one or two people.
Small saucepans are also among the more or less discarded articles
which can be revived, for with a spirit lamp they offer a convenient means of heating milk at table.

One of the 'revivals' which is particularly charming is the use
of the small tumblers for sherry.   The first we saw used in this
way were on a salver with a decanter which was surrounded by
these little bowls tinkling like merry bells as, empty, they wobbled
against one another; and after they were filled and emptied again
they were the source of considerable fun as small wagers were
made as to who could spin one for the longest time.   Several in
the party even ventured to compete with their tumblers half
filled with sherry.

Oblong snuff-boxes such as were made in the early nineteenth
century are of various sizes; the deeper ones have come into their
own again as cigarette boxes on the table beside a favourite chair
and the shallower ones for carrying in a hand-bag or in a man's
pocket.   If you come upon one with the musical attachment, it
is worth buying providing it is in working order, though it is
well not to allow too many strange hands to wind the mechanism
as it is somewhat delicate.

SECTION 4
Distinctive Features of Later Styles

CHAPTER NINE

FROM THE HIGH STANDARD TO THE EMPIRE

ENGLISH SILVERWORK of the eighteenth century may be divided into three distinct periods—namely, the high standard or Britannia, the rococo and the classic. The first two are related, because the rococo was an extension of the earlier designs to which French ornamental forms were grafted by the Huguenot silversmiths who came to England. Then after about 1765 silver developed an entirely new style under the guidance of Robert Adam who introduced and popularized the ancient classic forms, which were fashionable until the end of the eighteenth century. During the following twenty-five years, designs were evolved from the classic forms, and various 'novelities' made their appearance some of which were influenced by the so-called French empire style, though none of these enjoyed any great vogue. But each of the eighteenth- and the early nineteenth-century styles may be identified by its own characteristic features which, after a relatively short 'course of observation', become familiar.

HIGH STANDARD PERIOD

To express it somewhat poetically, we might describe the extravagant times of Charles II as the Rubicon crossed by the English silversmiths to the path leading to the golden era of their craft. This era opens with what we know as the high standard or Britannia period; a period when silverwork was distinguished by its fine shapes whose simple beauty was less affected by foreign influence than those of any other time.

Admittedly its simplicity was due more to necessity than to any demands of fashion for which perhaps we moderns should be grateful, because otherwise we might not have known the plain silver of that time. The necessity arose from the change in the standard of silver by the reduction in the amount of alloy as explained in an earlier chapter. To a layman it may seem strange that this change should affect the designs. But alloy is added to pure silver to harden it—not to save silver—and softer metal materially restricts the character of ornamentation, because as the silversmiths recognized, any delicate details would quickly show signs of wear.

Therefore the typical decorative forms of the high standard period are cut-card work, both plain and pierced, flutings, applied gadroon, punched leaf outlines and, with larger pieces, cast shells, masks, animal and human figures, and handles with terminal figures.

With the more elaborate silverwork there is patent evidence of that French influence which was introduced by the Huguenot silversmiths who had fled to England to escape persecution when the Edict of Nantes was revoked by Louis XIV in 1685. And, as we shall 'see, these men were later to introduce to England a style of silver which at times developed a fantastic and wholly un-English character.

Though plain forms predominated no austerity prevailed in the early eighteenth century. This is evident from the huge wine fountains and cisterns which were to be found in the dining-room of all large houses. The fountain which, as a rule, was about 3 feet high was similar to a large vase with two handles and fitted with a tap from which the wine was drawn in the same way as tea is drawn from an urn; the cistern was oval, about 3 feet long with two ornamental handles. In their own time, the cisterns served the same purpose as wine coolers do to-day—namely, to hold ice and water in which the bottles of wine were placed to cool until needed.

These imposing objects were variously decorated with gadrooning, flutings, foliage and chased work and the handles were in the form of female figures, dragons, lions' heads and similar cast ornaments.

Toilet sets of thirty or more pieces continued to be widely fashionable as gifts inspired by the love of a lady. As an example of the variety of articles which would comprise some of these beautiful sets we might quote one made by Benjamin Pyne, hall-marked 1708–9, which was sold at Christie's in 1947. In addition to a large mirror in a moulded silver frame with a shaped pediment, it included: a small helmet-shaped ewer and basin, a pair of candlesticks, a pair of oval bowls with covers, three oblong caskets, four circular boxes and covers, a pair of small covered cups with handles, a pair of small tazze, a pair of vases and covers, a pair of tray candlesticks and a snuffer tray with snuffers, a pair of glass bottles with silver-gilt covers, hair brushes, whisks and a table bell. Truly a magnificent array on a sufficiently large dressing table.

Many of these sets have been preserved by succeeding generations who have descended from the different ladies to whom they were given originally; but modern so-called progress and the financial stress it brings frequently demands that they be exchanged for that necessity money, and the past few decades have seen all too many brought into the auction room and pass into strange hands.

But even if there was some display in the larger houses of the fashionable world in the days of Queen Anne, it was much more restrained than in the time of Charles II. Rather, it was a time when homes, as we know them, were being established and the silversmiths were engaged in making silver for everyday use. Consequently, that which has come down through the years from the early eighteenth century has more of personal and less of historical associations. Moreover, it undoubtedly represents a quality and skill unsurpassed at any period before or after.

Trade with the outside world was increasing and those interested in commerce began to gain in wealth and social importance. And the increasing power of those concerned with trading at this time is illustrated by the failure of Queen Anne's ministers to exclude merchants from sitting in the House of Commons in 1711.

These importers and exporters, as we would call them, were

the founders of that great body of people known to-day as the
middle classes.   And as their material prosperity raised them on
the social ladder, they naturally began to increase the luxury of
their domestic surroundings, which in turn added to the prosperity of the cabinet-maker, the weaver and the silversmith.

Important as this stimulus was, however, the silversmiths
enjoyed a more powerful one from the various exotic foods and
drinks that were brought to England in always increasing quantities from the Far East.   Tea, coffee and chocolate, which had
been introduced to England some years before, became widely
popular during the time of Queen Anne and this brought a
demand for silver vessels suitable for serving these drinks and for
the accompanying milk and sugar.

Casters, which were known in the late seventeenth century,
came into general use and plain cast candlesticks with simple but
attractive baluster stems were made in fairly large numbers (see
Figs. 42 and 44).   The great standing-salts were forgotten, but a
relic of them remained for a few years in a circular trencher salt
about 2½ inches high with a wide spreading base rather like the
shape of a trumpet; but most of the salt-cellars were the attractive
little trencher types either octagonal (Fig. 29), circular or oval
shaped.   Other silver for the dinner table included sauce-boats,
broth-bowls, soup-tureens and spoons and forks, which are
described fully in later chapters.

On rare occasions, too, one of the splendid services of silver-
gilt dishes will appear in the auction room; but to enjoy the
possession of one calls for a more than average bank balance.

All the silver which was intended for general use relied for its
beauty upon its simplicity of outline.   None evinces any suggestion of severity, and light and shade effects were obtained both by
the skilful use of fine mouldings and faceting and the introduction
of angles to the shapes.   For instance, some of the little octagonal
trencher salts were made with as many as six varying mouldings
or members, as they are known technically.   Again, pear-shaped
articles such as tea-pots, coffee-pots and casters would be hammered up with eight sides and a small moulding applied round the
shoulder and the rim (Fig. 7).   One tea-pot of the pear outline

with twelve sides which was made in Dublin, 1715, is in the Victoria and Albert Museum.   And straight-sided tapering coffee and chocolate-pots with the flat moulded bottom were also made with eight sides (Fig. 21).

Wine-glasses came into general use, consequently there were fewer silver vessels associated with the age-old pastime of drinking.   The small two-handled cups called porringers were made but within a few years they too went out of fashion.   The large tankards with the slightly tapered body and the flat cover remained popular for a few years, then were gradually replaced by a less imposing type with a more pronounced taper, a moulded rib round the body and a domical cover.

There still exist a fair number of large two-handled cups which recall Queen Anne's enthusiasm for horse-racing.   Some of them were given by her for a particular race in which she competed with her own horses which were run in her own name.   Several of the cups given by this sporting Queen were of gold and one of these came up at Christie's in 1929 when it was bought by S. J. Phillips for £5,000.

It is 9 inches high and quite plain with a moulded rib round the bowl and a domical cover and scroll handles.   On one side it is engraved with the royal arms and cypher of Queen Anne and on the reverse with a racehorse and jockey and the inscription, *Ruffler and Woodcock on Braham Moor, 1705 and 1708* which so far as we can discover was a race-meeting held in Yorkshire. Three others of this period in the same sale were of silver, the Saltby Free Plate cup, 1708, and the Kiplingcoates cups for 1702 and 1709.

There is little doubt that a large number of plain cups with covers were made in England for racing trophies during the first quarter of the eighteenth century; and similar cups were produced in Ireland, but the latter were mostly without covers.

And it may here be of interest to recall some of the numerous races which came into being as a result of the encouragement that horse-racing received from Queen Anne.   Doncaster races were established in 1703, York in 1709 and in the following year Queen Anne gave a gold cup which was run for by six-year-olds carrying 12 stone. Two years later, one of the Queen's own horses was entered for the Royal Cup and another of her stable ran for the same prize in 1713. It was at this time, too, that Newmarket began to come into prominence and it was here that Basto, one of the earliest race-horses recorded, won several races in 1708 and 1709.

Two-handled cups of the type described above are frequently spoken of as loving-cups, the two handles allowing for the passing of the cup 'to drinke crosse one to ye other' as a token of goodwill; and it is not difficult to imagine that having won a race, the winner would be called upon to fill his trophy often and 'drinke crosse' to many.

Small beer mugs, presumably for those with a smaller capacity

FIG. 5. Plain tapered mug.
Newcastle, 1793. H. 5 in.

for this popular drink, seem to have come into use about the end of the seventeenth century and a number of attractive types were made from the high standard period to the late eighteenth century (Fig. 5). They are from 3 inches to 4 inches high of the straight tapering shape copied from the contemporary tankards and have a similar flat moulded bottom. Most of them have the stout hollow S-scroll handle which was also copied from the tankards, but this is sometimes replaced by scroll-shaped strip of sheet silver ribbed to stiffen it.

Though some were made quite plain, they were mostly ornamented by various styles of fluting, punched work or bands of chased lines round the body; and not infrequently a narrow

band or rib was applied round the upper part of the body.
While it cannot be said these little mugs are numerous, examples
do come on offer, though their popularity among collectors has
caused their value to rise noticeably in recent years.

Snuff-taking which became fashionable in the time of Queen
Anne added further to the prosperity of the silversmiths who were
called upon to make the delightful little boxes of which more
will be said in a later chapter.

THE ROCOCO PERIOD

During the two hundred years from the appearance of the
Renaissance influence in the first quarter of the sixteenth century,
English silverwork reverted periodically from highly ornamental
to plain.   As we have seen, the raising of the standard of silver
brought a period of relatively plain designs and, after the old
standard (harder) metal was restored in 1720, decoration again
became fashionable.

This new fashion is directly traceable to the large number of
French Huguenot silversmiths who came to England and Ireland;
some two hundred of these skilled craftsmen settled in London
and English provincial centres and at least as many in Dublin in
addition to those who worked in Cork.

Plain silver continued to be popular until about 1725, but from
that time until the coming of the classic styles about forty years
later the French influence was predominant.   And the renewed
desire for magnificence and ostentation in fashionable circles was
expressed in silverwork which was elaborately and not infrequently fantastically ornamented.

France derived the rococo style from Chinese forms which were
developed to their asymmetrical exuberance by Juste-Aurele
Meissonier who was the director of the royal furniture factory in
Paris in the time of Louis XV. The ornamental forms he
designed for furniture were adapted to silver when the rococo
became fashionable in France and were brought to England by
the Huguenot silversmiths, the more prominent of whom were
the celebrated Paul De Lamerie and Liger, Blanchard, Harrache,

Le Sage, Mettayer, Crespin, Courtauld, Archambo, Portal, Willaume, Platel, Buteux.

In England, these émigrés grafted rococo ornaments upon the simple forms of the high standard period and it is by these forms that silverwork of the rococo period may be identified. In France, it was known as *rocaille* (shell-work) and the dominant ornament is the shell which was combined with scrolls or gad-rooning on the borders of such pieces as salvers, trays, dishes, etc.; shell-work was also chased and embossed at the base of spouts and as fringing to scrolls; and among the many other decorative motifs were sprays of flowers, sea-monsters, tritons, animal heads, ribbons, symbolic figures such as Hope and Despair and various other more or less fantastic forms which were either embossed and chased or cast and applied to larger objects.

While we are not interested in the fanciful conceptions for use in a present day home, it is of interest to mention one or two of the extravagant pieces that were made during the rococo period and which have been preserved to the present time. A large number of these were made in the shop of Paul De Lamerie who sometimes allowed his imagination to overrule his sense of proportion in his profuse ornamentation and fantastic shapes.

There is a soup tureen by him in the form of a turtle on its back, the flippers being reversed to serve as feet and the head and small tail serving as handles; the movable cover is the flat belly shell and has a smaller turtle as a handle. Others are a pair of sauce-boats with a grotesque human mask on a large shell under the spout while the rest of the body and the foot are decorated with flowers, scroll-work foliage and grotesque masks and the handle is in the form of a dragon.

This by no means implies that all silver of the rococo period is of the character of that just described. In fact, such pieces are relatively few and most of the domestic silver readily finds a place in a modern home. Obviously the native English silver-smiths were compelled to produce work in the prevailing fashion, but, with few exceptions, their work was rarely as ornate as some made by their Anglo-French contemporaries.

As we have mentioned, the use of silver in the home was considerably extended in the first quarter of the eighteenth century, but this was far exceeded during the time of George II. Plates and large dishes, soup-tureens, sauce-boats in addition to the smaller pieces such as salt-cellars and casters came into general use not only in the large houses, but in more modest homes.   It was at this time too, that silver mustard-pots and the now discarded cruèt-frame were added to the table silver.   The favourite cruet-frame was the so-called Warwick which was fitted with three silver casters and two glass cruets with silver tops.

This extension of more luxurious appointments for the dinner table brought prosperity to the silversmiths; but they enjoyed an equal impulse from the always increasing demand for things necessary to the tea table.

During the forty years 1726–66 the amount of tea imported to Britain rose from 700,000 to 7,000,000 lb., due primarily to the reduction in the cost which meant that it was more widely used in middle class homes; and this is reflected in the number of silver tea-pots, cream-jugs, sugar-bowls and little tea-caddies which were made during the rococo period and which have been handed down to the present time.

There is another forgotten phase of tea-drinking which contributed largely to the demand for silver.   One of the fashionable customs was to meet for tea at public tea gardens which were established first in the early eighteenth century.   These places of summer amusement, as an old guide book calls them, eventually became so widely popular that the more cultured classes refused to patronize them and gathered together for tea and gossip in their own houses; and so the fashionable afternoon tea ceremony came into being.

Incidentally, the tea gardens remained popular for well over a century. Leigh's *New Picture of London* (1830) lists twenty-one which include: Chalk Farm, Primrose Hill; St. Helens Gardens, Deptford; Yorkshire Stingo, Lisson Green; and the Montpelier, Walworth. It was at the Montpelier that an eleven of one-armed and an eleven of one-legged pensioners played a game of cricket for a wager of a thousand guineas between two lords of the realm, but the longest lived were the famous tea-gardens at Vauxhall which closed in 1859.

Coffee would seem to have been more particularly favoured by men and while no 'coffee-gardens' were opened, coffee-houses became very numerous in London and other large centres. Chocolate was also served in the coffee-houses, but while this drink enjoyed a vogue in fashionable circles for some time, it was never as popular as coffee.

These coffee- and chocolate-houses were the clubs of their day and the names of several of the eighteenth-century proprietors have survived in those of some of London's well known clubs. For example, White's is descended from White's chocolate house which was opened first in 1698 and became the head-quarters of the Tory party; Brook's, is the offspring of Brook's coffee-house established in 1764 which was then the meeting place of the Whigs or Liberals as we now know them; and Boodle's which was opened in 1762 was later the club associated with country gentlemen.

There is an amusing reference to these meeting places in the *Spectator*: A correspondent writing from Cambridge asked for information regarding any members in London of a 'sect of Philosophers . . . called Lowngers' adding that he was 'compiling a Treatise wherein I shall set forth the Rise and Progress of this famous Sect'.

Steele, who replied to this inquiry, wrote:

When the Lowngers leave an Academick Life and instead of this more elegant way of appearing in the polite World, retire to the seats of their Ancestors, they usually join a pack of Dogs and enjoy their days in defending their poultry from Foxes . . . but I shall enquire into such about Town as have arrived at the dignity of being Lowngers by the Force of Natural Parts without having ever seen a University; and send my correspondent for the Embellishment of his Book the Names and History of those who pass their Lives without incidents at all; and how they shift coffee-houses and chocolate-houses from Hour to Hour to get over the insupportable Labour of doing nothing.

For a short time the pear-shaped tea-pots (see Fig. 7) that had been fashionable in Queen Anne's time continued to be made; but in place of being plain they were usually chased with rococo decoration. Most of the tea-pots, however, were of the globular shape (Fig. 8) with a straight or duck-neck shaped spout and either quite plain or decorated with restrained scrolls, shells and other forms on the shoulder and the edge of the lid. These tea-pots remained popular throughout the rococo period and are equally popular in our own time. About the middle of the eighteenth century, there was a reversion to the pear-shape, but now the bulbous part of the pear was above giving a wavy outline to the body.

Both coffee- and chocolate-pots retained some more or less distinct pear-shaped outline (Fig. 23). The same applies to the cream-jugs with the exception of the more fanciful conceptions produced by some of the Anglo-French silversmiths. Sugar-bowls which were quite small (about 4 inches diameter) were fitted with a cover (Fig. 15) and the tongs were similar to a pair of scissors. Tea-caddies were made in a variety of shapes and usually embossed and chased in the more elaborate rococo style.

It was during this period that the large centrepieces were introduced from France. These became fashionable as ornaments for the centre of the dining table and were in most instances modified versions of the massive *surtout de table* which, to an extent, would seem to have replaced the standing salt.

As a general rule, the English centrepieces while quite large are far less ornate than the French prototypes, as for example, one which was sold at Christie's a few years ago. This has a large centre dish fitted into a chased ring raised on brackets supported by a quatrefoil platform and four scroll legs. A candle-bracket is fitted into a socket on each of the four legs which alternate with four brackets, each holding a saucer and fitted into sockets fixed to the shaped platform.

Some of these great ornaments are equipped with casters and cruet bottles in addition to the various brackets holding saucers; and one of Paul De Lamerie's invoices includes the item 'a fyne polished surtout cruette frame, casters, branches and saucers weighing together 505 oz. 10 w.'   There is in the Victoria and Albert Museum an electrotype of one such centrepiece by De Lamerie which was formerly in the Bobrinsky collection at Moscow.   This is 32 inches long and 23 inches wide and affords some idea of the splendour of the table appointments in the early Georgian days.

Though we have referred to the large table ornaments described above, as centrepieces, they are also called epergnes. To-day, however, the name epergne generally refers to the more familiar and less masssive type which became popular after the revival of pierced work during the rococo period and are still used on present day tables.   For while one of the centrepieces would be too much for the average dining table, the pierced epergnes are neither as large nor as overpowering.

These epergnes and the beautifully pierced cake baskets (Fig. 41) of this time will be dealt with more fully in a later chapter.

The Adam or Classic Style

In about 1765, there was another radical change in the designs for domestic silver, and like those of the Queen Anne and earlier Georgian periods they were developed from ancient art.   For while those of the first part of the century were inspired largely by the Chinese forms, so those of the late Georgian or Adam period, as it is known in England, were based upon those of the Greco-Roman art.

This new style was the outcome of the discoveries at Herculaneum and Pompeii, both of which cities had been destroyed by the eruption of Vesuvius in A.D. 79.   Tentative excavations were made at Herculaneum as early as 1711, but it was not until 1738 that really serious work was begun and many objects of art and monuments of an early civilization were unearthed.

Some twelve years later, work was commenced on Pompeii, part of which was then cleared.   In 1763, organized excavations were started and numerous beautiful objects, among them articles of silver and bronze, were found among the ruins.

Within a short while, the results of these discoveries were published and the drawings resulted in a completely new fashion. This change appeared in France and other continental countries some few years before the influence of the classic art was accepted in England where the rococo was not superseded until about 1765.

We have said that the new fashion is generally known in this country as the Adam style. This is explained by its having been fostered by Robert Adam who was one of four sons of a Scottish architect. After spending some years in Italy studying ancient architecture he and his brother James established themselves as architects in London. But though primarily concerned with designing buildings, Robert Adam also published drawings of numerous objects necessary to the interior treatment of and for use in the mansions and houses built after his own classic designs.

Adam's influence upon silverwork of his time was exercised indirectly through the drawings he published. Indirectly, because the silversmiths, instead of copying the often pompous and formal conceptions, modified and adapted them to a style suitable for an average household rather than for the classic interiors of the large mansions. And the silversmiths exercised considerable ingenuity in their use of the various ornamental forms which they borrowed from Robert Adam's designs.

Ornamentation was invariably restrained and at no time did it overwhelm the outline of the article to which it was applied, as was frequently the case with the more exuberant rococo decoration. The Adam style is distinguished both by the predominance of the ovoid outline and certain well defined classic ornaments, among which are masks, rams' heads, lions' heads, festoons of drapery, acanthus and laurel leaves, beaded mouldings, figures, medallions enclosing classical subjects, usually embossed and chased (see Fig. 24).

Pierced work was used with trays (Fig. 65) and fruit and cake baskets, occasionally in the style of wicker-work but generally of geometric forms; similar pierced decoration is found with decanter stands or coasters as they are sometimes called, epergnes, sugar bowls, salt-cellars and other articles.

Candlesticks retained the baluster stem (see Figs. 42–44) for a short time, but within a few years the baluster gave place to a wide variety of types, many of which had the fluted column and capital inspired by the ancient classic architecture. With others, the shaft is formed of engaged columns borrowed from the Gothic (Fig. 49); others have a rectangular shaft with concave sides and there are yet other types which, with few exceptions, reveal a strong architectural inspiration.

Any study of the silver of this time reveals that there was far less made for display than in the rococo period and that both the designers and the makers concentrated upon producing articles for everyday use. Admittedly few modern dining-rooms would 'blend' with some of the pieces such as the massive soup-tureens and the more formally ornate objects among which some coffee-pots and jugs and candlesticks may be included; but even so, those same imposing examples are important as representing a time in the history of Britain when ideologies were unknown, or at least not recognized, and each went his way according to his wont.

There is no lack of later eighteenth-century silver suitable for present day use. It was a time when the less wealthy families knew that love of a home and the things around them which became and has remained so outstanding a characteristic of the British race. More articles were introduced for the dinner table; among them entree dishes with the detachable handle, others with a compartment to hold hot water to keep the contents of the dish hot, sauce-tureens with covers, argyles for holding gravy (see Figs. 53, 58 and 60), all came into general use. And if an urn is seldom required to-day except at large gatherings, it was during the Adam period that the silver tea-kettles were largely replaced by the silver tea-urn. These imposing objects were filled with boiling water or strained tea which was kept hot by a billet of hot iron placed in a socket inside the urn; others were fitted with a spirit lamp underneath.

During the time the Adam style was in vogue, the ancient vase shape predominated and was adapted to two-handled cups, coffee-pots, chocolate-pots (Fig. 24), jugs, sugar-bowls, cream-jugs and tea-caddies. The large two-handled cups, which were used as loving cups or as trophies for horse-races and other sporting events, are among the few silver objects which were intended more for display than for use.

These somewhat imposing pieces may be of small interest to those whom we might call collector-users, but they are well worth studying as examples of the classic forms and ornamentation. There are two in the Victoria and Albert Museum which might well serve for this study; each has the conical bowl following the outline of the Greek and Roman vases and the ornamental forms are equally typical of the classic style. One has a tall concave cover decorated with leaves with a vase-shaped finial, the bowl is also decorated at the base with leaves, and above with festoons of drapery suspended from masks and a band of vertical flutes round the rim.

The second two-handled cup illustrates other forms of classic ornament such as festoons of leaves pendant from ribbon knots, rosettes, running foliated scrolls and acanthus leaves on the cover and round the base of the bowl.

Attempts were made to adapt the conical vase-shape to teapots but the results were, to say the least, unsatisfactory, and an entirely different style of tea-pot was introduced during the latter part of George III's reign. In place of the curved outline, teapots were made straight-sided either circular, oval or octagonal (Fig. 11) with a straight tapering tubular spout, and were usually accompanied by a small stand on feet.

Summing up the various features which distinguish the silverwork of this period, we have the urn shape and the various classic ornaments which Robert Adam expressed in his drawings.

The Early Nineteenth Century

Soon after the opening of the nineteenth century, the classic or Adam style gave place to the so-called Empire designs which were introduced from France. One Frenchman defined the Empire style as the 'decorative style adopted in the time of Napoleon I which is characterized particularly by its sobriety and the severity of its lines'. Possibly he was sincere according to his own view-point, but it would impress most people in this country as pompous and pretentious. Nor would it be otherwise consider-ing that the designs were evolved to symbolize the greatness of Napoleon and to pander to his egoism.

Our French friend's suggestion that the Empire style is notice-able for sobriety is by no means supported by the ornamental forms for which the designs reached back to ancient Rome and Greece and added a considerable quota borrowed from Egypt. The list of these is long, but the principal ones are the acanthus and laurel leaves, the Greek fret, beaded borders, rosettes, festoons, fluting, human heads and masks, the lotus, legs with cloven or lion feet, winged busts, the lyre and cornucopia. And candlesticks were made with the shaft in the form of an Egyptian mummy and in larger objects, figures of Roman soldiers, swans, snakes and dolphins were often introduced.

While the more extravagant Empire designs were repeated in this country, the few examples that exist are patently foreign and un-English. The style was adopted fairly widely with furniture and enjoyed some popularity, but the silversmiths soon recog-nized that it was unsuitable for the metal they worked in.

Various artists, among whom Thomas Stothard and John Flaxman were prominent, produced designs in the Empire style which were intended to be executed in silver. Unfortunately, judging from the results of the silversmith's efforts, the skill of these artists with the pencil was far greater than their knowledge of the character of silver, at least as a medium by which to interpret many of the curious objects suggested by their imagina-tions.

Some interesting even though fantastic examples which were made after designs by Flaxman are in Windsor Castle and these show not only the remarkable imagination of the artist, but the prodigal waste of silver necessary to execute the designs. For example, a vase and pedestal which measure nearly 30 inches high and weigh over 763 oz.; the vase, which was made in 1780-1, is itself extravagant, but is surpassed by the pedestal which was made thirty-five years later.

This pedestal is a typical example of the incongruities so often achieved by the early nineteenth-century artists when they allowed their fantasies to run riot—as they often did. It rests on eight dolphins each about 10 inches long and rises in a conglomerate mass on a shaped platform with a cupid lying and holding a chain attached to a large swan at each corner; and so that no part of this massive affair was left unadorned, large acanthus leaves were added and at the base a shell and a beaver.

Though the French interpretations of the Empire style were occasionally slavishly reproduced by English silversmiths, we may decide that these were too stiffly formal to be accepted. Some tea services and other objects of this character do exist, but even when any appear it cannot be said they attract any great interest.

Certain designs which were modified forms of the French styles enjoyed some slight vogue during the early nineteenth century, but most of these lack the character we look for in our household silver. For instance, a tea-pot rather like a shallow basin fitted with a large handle and short spout was one of the shapes introduced from France and services with a similar tea-pot were made in England.

Yet whatever opinion we may individually hold of the Empire style, it has to be recognized as the last with a real artistic parentage. For when its short life had ended, design wandered helplessly toward the threshold leading to that desert of experiment in which it has since called aloud for a leader. The machine was taking the place of the man and silverwork, like other crafts, was soon to lose that individual character which distinguishes the handicraft of the skilled artist-craftsman from the monotonous precision of the machine.

Another adverse influence sprang from the invention of electroplating which, coming into practical use in about 1840, not only supplanted fused or, as it is better known, Sheffield plate, but introduced what was, in truth, mass production; and the craftsmen had to compete with machine-made shapes of base metal disguised by a thin deposit of silver and the importance of quantity superseded the pride of quality.

Nevertheless, there are many articles of household silver of the early nineteenth century and since, which were made by those men of or descended from the old school who remained loyal to traditional design and unaffected by novelties or those contorted objects which have been paraded as 'modern design'.

CHAPTER TEN

SPOONS, FORKS AND KNIVES

WHEN MAN LEARNED to make semi-liquid food, it would seem likely that he scooped it to his mouth with a piece of wood. This suggestion finds support in the derivation of the word spoon which comes from *spon*, a chip. Then finding this inconvenient, he bethought himself of a shell and later, as he developed cutting tools, made spoons with bowls of horn, wood and bone.

It is not possible to say when spoons were first made of metal, but there are several references to gold spoons in the Old Testament. In fact, the Book of Exodus alone would indicate that metal working had reached a high degree of development even at that early age.

Here we need not touch at any length upon the early history of man's first eating tool. But it is of interest to mention that shapes of the bowls of ancient Greek and Roman spoons are to be found in those of different later periods to the present time. Thus until about the middle of the seventeenth century English spoons had the fig-shaped bowl, after which it became elliptical which, in turn, developed to the egg-shape and later still to a more pointed end.

Though our present interest is directed particularly to silver-work of the eighteenth century, we will travel back as far as the days of Cromwell and follow the evolution of the spoon from the rather crude type called the Puritan which has been described in Chapter Six. After about 1660, the end of the stump stem was widened, then it was rounded and a small notch or cleft made at each side of the top which was the forerunner of the trifid pattern. With the last mentioned, the stem was made thinner, and widened at the end to an outline rather like a pear-shape which was notched on each side of the top in such a way as to leave a small tongue-like section which turned up toward the face of the bowl (see fork, Fig. 6B, *1*).

Various changes appeared in spoons during the last few years

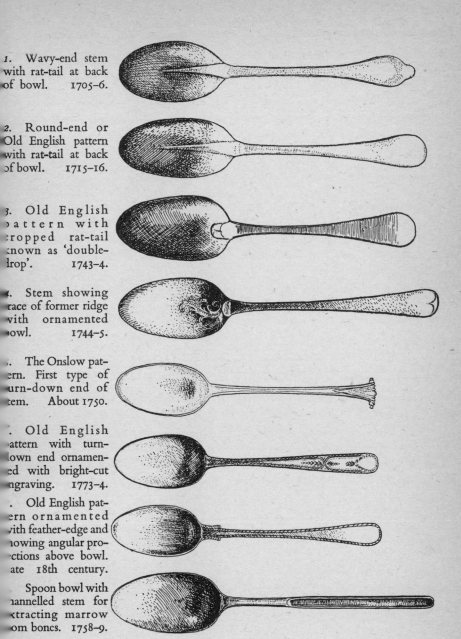

1. Wavy-end stem with rat-tail at back of bowl. 1705–6.

2. Round-end or Old English pattern with rat-tail at back of bowl. 1715–16.

3. Old English pattern with cropped rat-tail known as 'double-drop'. 1743–4.

4. Stem showing trace of former ridge with ornamented bowl. 1744–5.

5. The Onslow pattern. First type of turn-down end of stem. About 1750.

6. Old English pattern with turn-down end ornamented with bright-cut engraving. 1773–4.

7. Old English pattern ornamented with feather-edge and showing angular projections above bowl. Late 18th century.

8. Spoon bowl with channelled stem for extracting marrow from bones. 1758–9.

FIG. 6. Spoons.

of the seventeenth and the early eighteenth centuries. The notches at the end of the trifid pattern became less noticeable and were often incorporated with decoration; then they disappeared and the pattern known as the wavy-end became popular—this is somewhat similar to the outline of the tops of some contemporary wall mirrors.

This wavy-end (Fig. 6, *1*) was the immediate ancestor of the spoons which are in everyday use in our time. Like its predecessor, it started life with a flat stem which was afterwards rounded about halfway up from the bowl, but the top retained its original flat shape. Another change was in the bowl which was made narrower and slightly more pointed; and at about this time the small section at the top of the stem between the clefts was hammered down to produce a semi-circular or rounded top with an unbroken curve.

This hammering down of the end may have been experimental in the first place, but it seems to have suggested the stem with the rounded top and the definite ridge down the face of the stem which is known as the Old English pattern. But while the latter lost other characteristics of its seventeenth-century ancestors, it retained the V-shaped tongue or rat-tail, as it is known, at the back of the bowl (Fig. 6, *2*).

In about 1730, the rat-tail was replaced by a small molded drop not unlike a cropped rat-tail with the result that the stem at the back of the bowl appears to have two drops, for which reason spoons of this type are often referred to as 'double-drop' (Fig. 6, *3*). Later in the reign of George II, the ridge down the stem was discontinued, except for a trace of it just below where the end turns up toward the face of the bowl (Fig. 6, *4*). And while during the later eighteenth century, the end of the stem was made to turn down and the face of the stems was engraved (Figs. 6, *6* & *7*), the original shape of the Old English pattern remained until the coming of the fiddle and the various other patterns which were fashionable in the early nineteenth century.

One other pattern which was made in the eighteenth century and enjoyed a certain vogue was called the Onslow pattern after Arthur Onslow, who was Speaker of the House of Commons from 1728 to 1761. The end of the Onslow stem finished in an ornamental volute scroll which curled under (Fig. 6, 5); and, the convenience of this being recognized, the turned down stem was in time adopted in the Old English pattern and those which followed it. So if the Onslow pattern was short-lived and is now almost forgotten, it did give us the more comfortable turned down stem—those who have used a fork with a turned-up stem-end will appreciate the difference.

During the later eighteenth century, the Old English pattern was sometimes made with a small angular projection on each side of the stem near the bowl—these projections are known as shoulders (Fig. 6, 7). This was the embryo form of the later fiddle pattern which with its more ornamental offsprings, the threaded edge and thread and shell, are in fairly general use in modern homes.

If perhaps little known to-day, there is one member of the

Fig. 6, 9. Marrow-scoop. About 1730.

spoon family which, as mentioned in a previous chapter, still has its uses, namely the marrow scoop. These have a long spoon-like bowl with a narrow channelled stem and in earlier days were used for scooping the marrow from bones (Fig. 6, 9). Some of them have a large spoon bowl with the channelled stem, but this type is rare (Fig. 6, 8).

FORKS AND KNIVES

Compared with spoons, forks are relatively newcomers, for they did not join the table silver until the later seventeenth century. A form of silver fork was known many centuries before, but these were primitive affairs with two small prongs at one end of the stem and a spoon bowl at the other. In early sixteenth-century inventories, they are referred to as a 'spone with a suckett fork uppon one stele' and were used when eating the dainties known as suckets which were plums, ginger or other fruit in a thick syrup. And though suckets are long since forgotten the name survive in 'sucker', the one-time name for a lollipop or sweet.

Various references to forks are to be found in books written by seventeenth-century travellers; and here it may be of interest to quote from Thomas Coryate's account of his walking tour in Europe which was published in 1611 under the title, *Coryate's Crudities hastily gobbled up in Five Months Travels in France, Italy, &c.*; and the comments of an Italian count upon English customs over fifty years after the *Crudities* appeared.

After remarking that Italy was the only country in which he had observed the custom, Coryate wrote:

The Italian and almost all strangers who are commorant in Italy doe alwaies at their meales use a little forke when they cut the meate; for while with their knife, which they hold with one hand, they cut the meate out of the dish, they fasten their forke, which they hold in their other hand upon the same dish. . . . This form of feeding I understand, is generally used in all places of Italy, their forkes being for the most part made of yron or steele, and some of silver, but those are used only by gentlemen. The reason of this their curiosity is, because the Italian cannot by any means indure to have his dish touched with fingers seeing all men's fingers are not alike clean. . . .   I myselfe thought good to imitate the Italian fashion by this forked cutting of meate . . . oftentimes in England since I came home. . . .

But though Coryate imitated the 'forked cutting of meate' it was not until long afterwards that silver forks were generally adopted in this country.

In fact, table manners seem to have been still somewhat crude in the time of Charles II judging from the observations of the Italian count who visited England at that time.   He wrote:

On the English table, there are no forks nor vessels to supply water for the hands, which are washed in a basin full of water, that serves for all the company or perhaps at the conclusion of dinner, they dip the end of the napkin into the beaker which is set before each of the guests, filled with water and with this they clean their teeth and wash their hands.

As explained in Chapter Six, it was still customary for a guest to bring his own table tools even as late as the time of William III; and the silversmiths produced several ingenious combinations suitable for carrying in the pocket. For example, a silver fork would have a spoon bowl (without a stem) as a companion

FIG. 6A. Combination spoon, fork, with toothpick in the end of the stem, for carrying in the pocket. Seventeenth century.

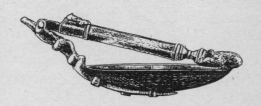

(Fig. 6A). The fork which was about 6 inches long with three prongs was hinged to fold and the ornamental end was attached to a tooth-pick which screwed into the top of the stem. The spoon-bowl had small loops fixed to the back in which the prongs of the fork could be fitted. In this way the combination could be used either as a fork or a spoon and when carried in the pocket, the stem could be folded to make it more compact. The later pocket cases containing a fork, spoon and knife were referred to earlier.

No really graceful fork appeared before the time of Queen Anne when the finely balanced three prong with the wavy-end stem was fashionable until it developed to the Old English shape which has been described with the contemporary spoons; and from then on, the stems of the forks follow the same patterns as the spoons. By the reign of George II, forks were larger and, in time, a distinction was made between table and dessert forks: by the second half of the eighteenth century, the heavy four-pronged table fork had replaced the earlier three prong.

Early knives with steel blades and pistol-shaped silver handles offer no attraction to the collector-user. These first made their appearance quite early in the eighteenth century and with their companion forks which had steel prongs, were still used in some houses until relatively recent times. Both the table knives and the forks are ungainly 'weapons' and some of us can remember having used them—it was similar to trying to eat with an ordinary carving knife and fork; the knives are about 12 inches long with a blade curved rather like a scimitar.   But if now unsuitable for use as dinner knives, one of them is an efficient bread cutter, for the steel blade is of a quality that retains a satisfying keenness, which cannot always be said of the present-day knife.

I. Mazer with silver lip-band and (upper picture) engraved print, 1507–8. D. 7¾ in.

III. Engraved and embossed tankard, 1574-5. H. 8 in.

II Tiger-ware jug; silver mounts, *circa* 1560. H. 7 in.

IV. Chinese porcelain bottle-shaped wine jug with silver-gilt wolf-head spout, neck-band, cover and scroll handle. Late sixteenth century. Height with cover, 9 in.

V.   Oval shaving basin and jug, 1717–8.   Basin, W. 13½ in.; jug, H. 7½ in.

VI.   Rosewater-dish and ewer, 1618–9.   Dish, D. 19 in.; ewer, H. 11½ in.

VII. Beaker, 1600–1. H. 6½ in.   VIII. Cromwellian embossed porringer, 1658–9. H. 5½ in.

X. Tankard with measure pegs, 1675–6. H. 7¾ in.   X.   Goblet, 1626–7. H. 8¼ in.

XI. Toilet service with gadrooned borders and applied cypher, J.B., which was owned originally by Judith, daughter of Sir John Bridgeman, Bart., to whose order it was probably made by Anthony Nelme in 1691–2. Height of mirror with cresting, 29 in.

XII. Wine fountain with horse-head handles, 1708–9. H. 22 in.

XIII. Oval wine cistern *en suite* with the fountain above, 1712–3. L. 27 in.

XIV. One of a pair of pear-shaped jugs with short spout, plain scroll handle, acorn finial to lid and spout cover; engraved arms of Fairfax, 1704–5. H. 10½ in.

XV. Set of casters, Edinburgh, 1702–3. Heights, (1) 8¼ in.; (2) 6½ in.

XVI. One of a pair of Queen Anne sconces with cypher of Charles II, 1713–4. H. 20 in.

XVII. Oblong bread basket with pierced scalloped sides, 1731–2. L. 15 in.

XVIII. One of a set of four dishes by Paul De Lamerie, 1738–9. D. $5\frac{1}{2}$ in.

XIX. Dish engraved in the rococo style by De Lamerie, 1743–4. D. 9¾ in.

XX. Standish or inkstand with sand-caster, bell and inkpot, 1727–8. L. 10 in.

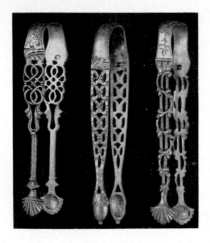

XXI. Pierced sugar tongs, *circa* 1760. XXII. Cow cream-jug, 1763–4. L. 5¾ in.

XXIII. Soup-tureen of the rococo period, eagle handle, 1745–6. H. 12 in.

XXIV. Kettle on stand with spirit lamp, pierced fringe, 1754–5. H. 15 in.

XXV. Pierced cake-basket with terminal bust handle, 1816–7. W. 13½ in.

XXVI. Two of a set of candlesticks by David King, Dublin, 1702–3. H. 10¼ in.

XXVII. Irish dish-rings of the three periods: Early
period, *circa* 1750. H. 3 in.; middle period, 1772. H. 4 in.;
and the more formal classic style, 1777. H. 4 in.

XXVIII. Chocolate-pot ornamented with cut-card work. The high domical lid is fitted with a small hinged lid to cover the hole for the molinet or stirring stick and a thumb-piece. By Robert Cooper, 1703–4. H. 10 in.

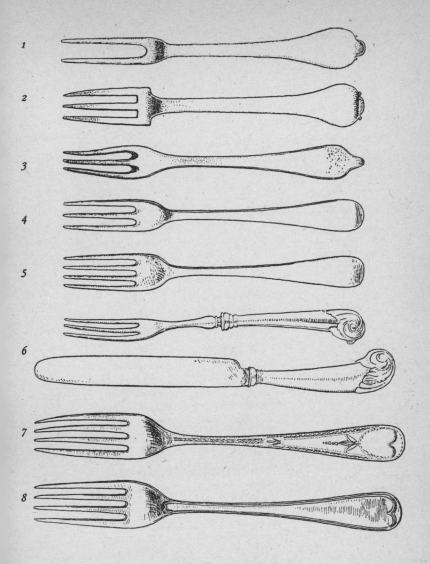

FIG. 6B. Types of 17th and 18th century forks. *1 & 2.* Trifid
stem. *3.* Wavy-end stem. *4.* Old English pattern, three
prong. *5.* Old English pattern, four prong. *6.* Pistol handle
fork and knife. *7.* Engraved bright-cut stem. *8.* Threaded edge.

CHAPTER ELEVEN

SILVER FOR THE TEA-TABLE

BEFORE WE TOUCH on the evolution of the many silver things that came to be associated with tea drinking, we might indulge in a few brief references to tea itself. For of all the various foods and drinks which began to find their way to Europe three hundred years ago, none became more popular or exercised the same influence on social life as tea.

First brought to Europe from the East by the Dutch in about 1610, it was not introduced to England until the latter years of the Commonwealth. At first, it was regarded as a medicine rather than a popular drink and was sold at from £6 to £10 a pound. In fact, it would seem to have been accepted as a cure for all ills that might afflict the human race, if the claims made for it by Thomas Garway are a criterion, for in an amusing broadsheet issued in 1659 or 1660, he claims for the 'fascinating plant' that:

It helpeth the headaches, giddiness and heaviness. It is very good against the stone and gravel. . . . It is good against lippitude distillations and cleareth the sight. It is good against crudities, strengthening the weakness of the stomach, causing good appetite and digestion particularly for men of corpulent body such as are great eaters of meat. . . . It is good for colds, dropsies and scurvies and expelleth infection. It prevents and cures agues, surfeits and fevers. . . .

There are many more physical troubles which, under the gentle stimulation of tea, would, according to Garway, disappear like the morning mists before the warmth of the sun.

Garway, who was the first English tea dealer, was doubtless aroused to this verbose enthusiasm by the fact that he had imported a large quantity of tea which he offered for sale at from 15s. to 50s. a pound according to quality. And though it became gradually cheaper, it was still expensive in the early eighteenth century and consequently restricted to the more wealthy people—in the time of George II, black tea was 13s. to 20s. a pound and green tea, 12s. to 30s.

There are several amusing recipes in contemporary literature for the proper brewing of tea, such as that of a distinctly religious character suggested by a missionary: 'To 1 pint of tea add yolks of 2 fresh eggs then beat them up with as much fine sugar as is sufficient to sweeten the tea and stir well.' And he adds that 'The water must remain no longer on the tea than while you can chant the Miserere psalm in leisurely fashion'.

With the importation of tea to Europe, the various articles of tea-ware used in China were also brought from the Far East. Much of this ware came from the Ihing (formerly Yi-hsing) potteries which produced a fine stoneware of different colours either plain or decorated with applied or incised designs. And the Ihing tea-pots were the models for the earliest European tea-pots which were made first in Holland and later in the seventeenth century by the Elers brothers in Staffordshire and Dwight at Fulham.

It is evident from the first silver vessel made in England to hold tea that the silversmiths were unfamiliar with the shapes of the Chinese tea-pots. The earliest known English tea-pot is a tall, tapering cylindrical affair, over 13 inches high, with a conical cover, a short tubular spout and a handle set at right angles with the spout. The body is the same outline as an inverted beaker, a shape more familiar to us in the table glasses we call tumblers; the first English silver tea-pot, like so many other articles, was therefore inspired indirectly by the ancient horn cups and was made in 1670; it is now in the Victoria and Albert Museum. At first sight it would be regarded more as a pot for coffee, but that it was intended for tea is clear from the inscription which reads, *This siluer tea Pott was presented to ye Comtte of ye East India Company.* . . . Within a few years, however, tentative efforts were made to copy the Chinese shapes and a few examples of the resulting, often quaint, tea-pots exist to the present time.

By the beginning of the eighteenth century, the pear-shape (Fig. 7) made its appearance. The outline of this shape had been used in the bowls of cups fifty years before, but the tea-pots of Queen Anne's time complete the shape of the fruit by the addition of a high domical cover.   The first pear-shaped tea-pots have the handle at right angles, but later the handle was in line with the spout.

FIG. 7.   Octagonal pear-shaped tea-pot
on stand with lamp.   1712–13.   H. 8 in.

At the same time, the globular shape (Fig. 8), copied from the little tea-pots that were brought from China, came into fashion and eventually superseded the pear-shape.   The early globular type are usually quite plain with a straight tubular spout; later they were decorated on the shoulder and the edge of the lid and the spout changed to the duck-neck shape which was cast and ornamented with fluted scrolls; the ornamentation was rarely profuse which probably accounts for the continued popularity of this attractive shape.

Actually there are very few English eighteenth-century tea-pots that are without a natural beauty; the reason for this is that the fine outlines are unspoiled by unnecessary decoration.   Admittedly freakish conceits were produced by some of the silversmiths, but even these are of interest if only as experimental attempts to 'paint the lily' and some of them are outstanding examples of fine embossed and chased work.

During the latter part of George II's reign, the pear-shape was revived, but now the wide part of the fruit was at the top, a

FIG. 8. Globular tea-pot with flush hinge to lid. 1748–9. H. 5 in.

'slice' of which was cut off and replaced by a flat or domed cover with a finial knob. Thus the pear instead of being in its natural position as it hangs from a tree, was inverted so that the small

FIG. 9. Plain inverted pear (pyriform) tea-pot. 1742–3. H. 5¾ in.

part was at the bottom, which explains why the shape is referred to as the inverted pear or, to use the more technical term, pyriform (Fig. 9). Like the globular tea-pots, some of these were plain but most of them are decorated with embossed and chased scrolls, leaf forms, flowers and other rococo motifs on the lid and on the upper part of the body, the ornamentation of the body extending, as a rule, down the sides.

In the latter part of the century, after the Adam style had

FIG. 10. Plain cylindrical (drum-shaped) tea-pot. 1774-5. H. 6 in.

FIG. 11. Engraved straight-sided tea-pot and stand.   1793-4.   H. 7 in.

ousted the rococo, tea-pots with curved outlines were superseded by those always desirable types with straight sides—in fact, these tea-pots are among the few objects of silver with vertical, horizontal and angular outlines which belong in the category of beautiful things (Figs. 10 and 11).

At first the straight-sided tea-pot was cylindrical or, as it is called, drum-shaped with a hinged flat lid and straight tubular spout (Fig. 10). These were flat-bottomed and without decoration; and it would not be wide of the mark to suggest that the later more attractive shapes were evolved from the simple drum-shape. It calls for little imagination to follow the several changes: the circular form was 'pulled out' to form an oval, from which it was a short step to shape the oval into an octagonal, or give it a wavy outline by flutings; for whatever the actual outline of the later eighteenth-century tea-pots, all of them are basically oval in plan and an oval is a close relative to a circle.

Nor would these variations offer any great difficulty to a craftsman, for, unlike the earlier pear and globular shapes which had to be raised from a flat circle of fairly heavy silver by patient and skilful hammerwork, the straight-sided tea-pots were thin sheet silver fashioned to the desired outline, the two ends being soldered together and a flat bottom soldered on. Even the spout is a plain tube which was cut from sheet silver, rolled round a suitable tool and soldered; yet this same simple spout is far more in keeping with the angular character of the body than the swan-neck shape which was adopted in about 1800. Some of the flat-bottom tea-pots are still accompanied by their little stand on four small feet (Fig. 11) which was intended to protect the table from the heat, but many have become separated during the years they have been in use.

Toward the end of the eighteenth century the straight sides of the tea-pots develop more or less pronounced curves and other variations were introduced. These will be described more fully with the tea services later in this chapter.

Any Oriental would insist that we Europeans spoil the flavour of tea by diluting it with cream or milk and it was, in fact, not until the early eighteenth century that the fashionable world in England decided that tea was more palatable when softened by the addition of milk. And so the silversmiths were called upon to design another vessel for the tea-table.

Having no knowledge of any other jug, the silversmiths at first copied the shape of the large helmet-shaped ewer which was used

FIG. 12.   Pear-shaped cream-jug with wavy rim. 1751–2. H. 3¾ in.

FIG. 14.   Helmet-shaped cream-jug with square plinth. 1806–7. H. 4½ in.

FIG. 13.   Cream-jug with chased decoration and bead-like punches round rim.   1780–1.   H. 3½ in.

to hold rose-water at the washing of hands, referred to earlier. And the first known jugs for cream or milk are helmet-shape on three legs similar to the Irish jugs (see Fig. 79). That does not suggest you should develop a desire for an English early eighteenth-century example, because they are very rare rarities.

Possibly the silversmiths realized that this style of small jug had no relation to the contemporary tea-pots, for in about 1730 the pear-shape was adopted and this in varying forms was popular for some forty years.

It was a time when plain silver was still fashionable and the silversmiths at first made the sturdy little pear-shaped jugs with the sharp beak-like spout on a low moulded foot from which the later variations were evolved. A few years later, the body became more definitely pear-shape and the moulded foot was replaced by three short legs; and in place of the applied spout, these have a long lip and the rim is cut to form a series of wavy curves. Some are quite plain (Fig. 12) but they were frequently chased with scrolls and flowers in the rococo style.

In about 1760, the fashion in cream-jugs was again changed and though the pear-shaped body and wavy rim were retained the three legs were replaced by a low stem and round moulded foot. Slightly later, with the introduction of the undulating or inverted pear-shaped tea-pots, the cream-jugs followed suit (Fig. 13). The latter have a somewhat taller foot than the preceding style and are usually decorated with embossed work, many of them having a row of bead-like punches round the rim to stiffen the metal (Fig. 13).

With the coming of the classic designs in the late eighteenth century, the pear-shaped jugs were superseded by the conical shape, often called helmet-shaped, with the long lip and loop handle (Fig. 14). These have a circular foot on a square or shaped plinth and, while attractive, are, like other silver of the time, somewhat formal and stiff compared with the earlier jugs.

When after about 1800, silverwork suffered from the experiments of the so-called designers of that time, the conical shape was reduced to a squat flat-bottomed jug with bulging sides and a helmet-shaped rim and angular handle. The only outstanding features of this shape are its entire lack of rhythmic outline and its resultant ugliness.

During the eighteenth century a number of fantastic cream-jugs were made by different silversmiths; and while few of them have any interest to the collector-user, we might here refer to the quaint goat and bee jug which is supposed to have been designed by Nicholas Sprimont, who was manager of the Chelsea porcelain works in addition to being a silversmith. This style of jug has a pear-shaped body decorated with flowers and leaves and on each side at the bottom a goat and a bee.

Another similarly quaint conceit is in the shape of a cow with its tail looped to form a handle. The cream is poured through the open mouth and the 'jug' filled through an opening in the back of the cow which has a small cover usually ornamented with a garland of tiny flowers and a bee in relief.

Whether tea was commonly sweetened in England before the time of Queen Anne is open to question, but the increase in the amount of sugar used during the second half of the seventeenth century would suggest that it was. Moreover, sugar was first refined in this country after about 1650.

Loaf sugar, as it is called, was invented at the end of the fifteenth century by a Venetian who conceived the idea of making it in the shape of a cone in a mould. An early reference to sugar loaves occurs in a letter of 1546 from Sir Edward Wotton to Lord Cobham saying that Sir Edward had bought twenty-five sugar loaves at 6s. each, 'whiche is eighte pence a pounde', from which we may infer that each loaf weighed 9 lb.

Loaf sugar was made in large moulds until fairly recent times and in old farmhouses you can still find the quaint sugar nippers with which the loaf was cut into small pieces. And until the last century, grocers still used three conical sugar loaves pendant as a shop sign.

Early eighteenth-century sugar-bowls were hemispherical and usually fitted with a cover which had a stout ring fixed to the top (Fig. 15). This style of bowl was undoubtedly copied from the Chinese porcelain bowls and it is probable that the ring on the cover served both as a handle and, if required, the cover could be inverted and used as a separate dish when the ring became a foot.

During the rococo period, the hemispherical bowl was replaced by the inverted pear-shape, most of which are somewhat extra-vagantly ornamented. Sugar-bowls of this latter shape were often one of a set with two equally ornate tea-caddies which were enclosed in a case covered with shagreen and mounted with silver. Various other styles of tea-caddies were made either singly and fitted with a lock (Fig. 17) or in sets of three in a case, but if of interest as specimens of eighteenth-century silverwork, they are of little use to-day unless, possibly, as ornaments.

Sugar-bowls of the Adam style often tended to be unnecessarily fanciful. Many of them were conical in shape of coloured glass

FIG. 15. Plain hemispherical sugar-bowl with cover. 1718–19. H. 3½ in.

FIG. 16. Plain boat-shaped sugar-bowl. 1798–9. L. 5¼ in.

FIG. 17. Engraved octagonal tea-caddy. 1788–9. H. 5½ in.

fitted into elaborately pierced silver cases embossed with various classical forms such as swags, and festoons of leaves. Others are boat-shape (Fig. 16) and these were not pierced, but usually decorated with bright-cut engraving; incidentally bright-cut is a series of zig-zag lines and, though more generally associated with the late eighteenth century, was a style of ornamentation used as far back as Anglo-Saxon times.

In the late eighteenth century sugar-bowls were made in the form of a classic vase with two handles. They are about 10 inches high and far too formal to find a place on a modern tea table, though one of them in a suitable setting is a beautiful ornament.

We have mentioned that loaf sugar was invented in the distant past and it was known in England at least by the time of Charles II. Silver sugar-tongs, however, do not seem to have been made here until the early part of the eighteenth century. The earliest were like a pair of scissors some of which had a shell-shape at the end of each blade to grip the sugar. Others of the scissor type were in the form of a stork, the long beak opening and gripping the sugar. Some of the latter might suggest that sugar was, in bygone days, associated with the legendary duty of the stork. Examples still exist in which, when the tongs are open, the figure of a baby is revealed inside the body of the stork and some of these 'baby-carriers' have a snake coiled round the neck of the bird; no explanation of the symbolism of the reptile, however, suggests itself.

Sugar-tongs of the more familiar bow-shape were made after the middle of the eighteenth century. The earlier ones which sometimes have the shell-shaped ends were finely pierced, but the later ones were decorated with bright-cut engraving or other designs to match the contemporary spoons. When the fiddle pattern became fashionable, sugar-tongs were shaped to match.

Tea-kettles, though considerably larger and on a stand with a spirit lamp, followed closely the shapes of the contemporary tea-pots. The earliest style was therefore the pear-shape of the early eighteenth century (Fig. 18). This was followed, in turn, by the globular, the inverted or undulating pear-shape (Fig. 19)

FIG. 18. Kettle on stand with pierced brazier. 1703–4. H. 14¾ in.

FIG. 19. Decorated pyriform kettle on stand with spirit lamp. 1747–8. H. 14½ in.

and in the early nineteenth century, adaptations of the classic and the various other experimental shapes of the tea-pots were repeated as kettles. As a general rule, they are accompanied by an ornamental stand with a spirit lamp, but occasionally the stand of the early examples was replaced by a brazier to hold charcoal, as in the case of the one illustrated in Fig. 18.

In the second half of the eighteenth century, the kettle was to some extent replaced by the large urns fitted with a small tap which then became fashionable. These massive pieces, which are upward of 24 inches high, were intended only for use at large gatherings when they were either filled with hot water or with strained tea which could be drawn off into the cups. The contents of the urn were kept hot either by a billet of hot iron, rather like a sash-weight, which was placed in a socket inside the urn, or by a spirit lamp underneath. But even if some of them when properly fitted serve as attractive table lamps, as part of a tea service they would be somewhat overpowering—though they do still come into use for their original purpose.

Tea-pots with the accompanying cream-jug and sugar-bowl of the same pattern were made before the time of George III, but it would mean a lengthy search and a not small outlay to obtain the three pieces each made by the same silversmith and bearing the same date letter.

Here we will confine ourselves to the later eighteenth- and early

FIG. 20.   Style of tea service fashionable during the late Georgian period.   Tea-pot 7 in. high.

nineteenth-century tea services of which there are many styles showing the later changes in the tea-pots and other things for the tea-table.   Were a vote taken to decide the more popular tea services, it is highly probable the majority would be for those with one of the straight-sided tea-pots accompanied by a conical cream-jug and boat-shaped sugar-bowl which date around 1790.

Some few years later there are signs of the departure from the straight sides and tea-pots develop a slight convex or outward curve and the straight spout is replaced by the swan-neck shape; and the graceful conical cream-jug and sugar-bowl on the high foot give way to the squat flat-bottomed style (see Fig. 20). This later tea-pot was developed from the straight-sided style of the Adam period and this influence continued into the early nineteenth century.   By then, however, the tea-pots assumed a more pronounced outward curve, and while the boat-shaped sugar bowl was used sometimes, the cream-jug is often a small bulbous affair without any sense of graceful line.

English tea services in the Empire style are few and far between. The probable explanation is that their foreign character failed to attract any more popularity at the time they were made than they have done since. It may be of interest, however, to describe one which came to the writer's notice. It comprised the usual three pieces and a hot water jug. Each of them is a dumpy bulbous shape ornamented round the lower part with flutings, a band of foliated scrolls and small flowers round the middle of the body and a row of large beads just below a series of flutes on the rim. The handles are ornamented with acanthus leaves and the upper socket is in the form of a female head; the jug is raised on an elaborate tripod with a platform below to take a spirit lamp— in brief, a waste of silver to produce a meaningless jumble.

CHAPTER TWELVE

COFFEE-POTS, CHOCOLATE-POTS AND JUGS

PROHIBITION RARELY achieves its object, but rather stimulates human curiosity and disobedience. We know something of inhibitive regulations in our time, but similar and even more amusing repressive enactments were inflicted in past eras. To-day, it is difficult to imagine that coffee was at one time banned as an evil by those who, like some modern self-appointed preceptors, decided that what they disliked was not good for others.

One petition against it by the women of 1674 claimed that 'it made men as unfruitful as the deserts whence that unhappy berry is said to be brought; that the offspring of our mighty ancestors would dwindle into a succession of apes and pigmies; and on a domestic message, a husband would stop by the way to drink a couple of cups of coffee.'

Coffee seems to have been brought to England from the Near East during the Commonwealth and it has been suggested it was then served in the bottle-shaped pottery vessels with a bulbous body and spout which also came from the Near East; this is probable as this shaped coffee-pot appeared on the tokens issued by some of the coffee-houses. The first known silver pot for coffee is hall-marked 1681–2 and is in the Victoria and Albert Museum. It is similar to the tall tapering tea-pot described in the preceding chapter, the only differences being with the handle which is set in line instead of at right angles with the spout and it is smaller than the tea-pot.

This straight-sided tapering style with the tall conical cover continued popular until the end of the seventeenth century, though the shape was made in the following century. During the Queen Anne and early Georgian periods, the same tall taper-ing shape with a flat bottom was retained, but it then became noticeably more refined. The former pointed cone-shaped lid developed to a high dome with fine mouldings and a baluster finial while the tubular spout was replaced by the graceful swan-neck shape (Figs. 21 and 25).

Some of the early eighteenth-century coffee-pots with the tapering body were made eight-sided with a domical lid and slightly heavier mouldings round the base (Fig. 21); and with this shape the lid would often be taller though octagonal and show a decided resemblance to the early conical lid.

While the pear-shape was adapted to tea-pots from the beginning of the eighteenth century, the straight-sided coffee-pots remained fashionable until the early part of George II's reign. And even though the pear-shape was adopted eventually, the change from the straight-sided style was noticeably gradual; the first sign of the pear-shape being a slight rounding of the flat bottom and the use of a moulded foot (Fig. 22).

About the middle of the eighteenth century, coffee-pots assumed the complete pear-shape which at first was plain apart from the cast spout ornamented with scrolls and other forms (Fig. 23), but later was often extravagantly decorated with embossed and chased designs. This shape was doubtless derived from the Chinese porcelain ewers of which there are examples in the British Museum.

Some few years later, the lower part of the pear was made more bulbous and the bottom 'pulled out' in a wavy outline to form what is called the undulating pyriform. This became fashionable during the later rococo period and more often than not the graceful shape was lost beneath the mass of scrolls, flowers and other unnecessary ornamentation.

With the introduction of the classic designs, all traces of the rhythmic curves of the pear disappeared and were superseded by coffee-pots fashioned after the Roman vase. These have a conical body on a high foot with a long concave neck, domical cover and elaborate spout. But the spout is modest compared with the remaining decoration which consists of a superabundance of festoons, swags, acanthus leaves, flutes and various other ornaments beloved of Robert Adam (see Fig. 24). Doubtless they were 'at home' against the formal magnificence of the classic

FIG. 22. Straight-sided coffee-pot with cast and chased spout. 1740–1. H. 9½ in.

FIG. 21. Plain octagonal coffee-pot. 1728–9. H. 10½ in.

FIG. 23. Plain pear-shaped coffee-pot with cast and chased spout. 1746–7. H. 9 in.

FIG. 24. Chocolate-pot of the Adam period. 1796–7. H. 12 in.

interiors, but one of them would certainly be 'unhappy' in any average modern setting.

Chocolate-pots of the earlier part of the eighteenth century are similar in shape to the contemporary coffee-pots. They can be distinguished, however, by an additional small cover hinged to the lid (Fig. 25) or a cork-like cylinder fixed to a flange.   These small additions closed the hole through which the stirring rod or molinet, as it was formerly known, was inserted to stir the chocolate.   In some instances, a small sliding disk is attached to the finial knob.   One side of the disk is riveted to the cover and

FIG. 25.   Chocolate-pot with the additional small hinged cover to lid.   1706-7.   H. 10½ in.

the opposite side has a small catch which slides under a stud to keep it closed firmly.

Jugs with hinged covers seem to have been in fairly common use throughout the eighteenth century.   They are similar to the pear-shaped coffee- and chocolate-pots, but have a short spout or lip applied to the rim in place of the longer spout.   It is probable they were used to hold chocolate, hot water or even beer and any one of them is equally useful to-day.

When the classic fashion replaced the rococo, the chocolate-pots which served equally as hot-water jugs took the Roman vase shape and were ornamented in the same style as the coffee-pots described above.   Instead of the long spout, however, they were fitted with a shaped rim and long lip, as shown in the example illustrated in Fig. 24.

CHAPTER THIRTEEN

PUNCH-BOWLS, MONTEITHS AND WINE-COOLERS

BY THE TIME at which our present interest begins, wine glasses had been generally adopted and the former silver cups and goblets were no longer fashionable. But if this meant work lost to the silversmith, he was compensated by the demand for other vessels connected with drinking, among them the large bowls for punch and the wine-coolers to hold a single bottle which took the place of the huge wine cisterns.

Punch was one of the several drinks which were introduced to England in the seventeenth century. It was brought from India and is generally thought to have derived its name from the Hindustani word *panch* (five), because originally it had five principal ingredients, i.e., spirit, spice, water, sugar and an acid from some fruit such as lemon or lime. Purists may object to this definition, but it is accepted tentatively by the lexicographers and in any event it is romantic.

From the time of Charles II to the early nineteenth century, at least one of these large silver bowls was to be found in every moderately wealthy home. Perhaps in these more austere days, they are rarely used for their intended purpose, but it is difficult to imagine a more beautiful table centre than one of them filled with various flowers.

While many had plain moulded rims and the bowls themselves were left plain, a large number were made with deep notches in the rim which was ornamented with applied scrolls and cherub heads, while the bowl was embossed with scrolls, flutes or otherwise decorated. The notched rim which is often movable was supposedly introduced by a Scotsman named Monteigh or Monteith and the bowls with this feature (Fig. 26) are still known as monteiths as distinct from punch-bowls with a fixed rim.

One early reference to these imposing vessels was made by Anthony Wood, the seventeenth-century antiquary in *Life and*

Fig. 26. Monteith bowl with removable rim. 1702-3. H. 8½ in. D. 12 in.

Times where, speaking of the year 1683, he says: 'This yeare in the summer time came up a vessel or bason notched at the brim to let drinking glasses hang there by the foot, so that the body or drinking place might hang in the water to cool them. Such a bason was called a "Monteigh" from a fantastical Scot called "Monsieur Monteigh" who at that time or a little before, wore the bottom of his cloake or coate so notched'.

Presumably, when the monteith was brought to the table, the glasses were taken out and the rim removed, thus leaving a bowl with a plain rim for brewing punch. During the past twenty or more years an appreciable number of these handsome pieces have passed through the auction rooms, but to own one calls for a fairly good reserve of liquid assets.

There are two small but important silver articles connected with the brewing of punch—namely the long handled ladle and the strainer. The ladles which were for filling the jugs from the bowl were made in large numbers, because they were used both with the porcelain and silver punch-bowls. These are still fairly plentiful and are as useful to-day as they were when they were first made—even if we suffer from a shortage of suitable liquid ingredients for punch.

FIG. 27. Pear-shaped beer-jug with cast scroll handle. 1761-2. H. 8½ in.

Strainers, on the other hand, are relatively scarce. The more common type was a perforated cup with two wire handles long enough to rest on each side of the punch-bowl; but the more desirable and therefore rarer kind had finely pierced and shaped handles.

Silver jugs (Fig. 27) that were probably used for serving punch, wine or beer in Georgian days were about 9 inches high and similar in shape to the first little pear-shaped cream-jugs. Examples are by no means plentiful, but they do come up for sale occasionally and are generally catalogued as beer-jugs.

Wine-coolers, fitted with a movable ice chamber, to hold a

FIG. 28. Vase-shaped wine-cooler on stand. 1808-9. H. 11 in.

single bottle (Fig. 28) were introduced during the first few years of the high standard period. From the time they first appeared, they retained the same general form of a large vase on a low foot and though the decoration varies according to the period at which they were made, they were invariably ornamented rather profusely.

They seem to have been particularly popular during the early nineteenth century and examples dating from that time are still fairly plentiful; but like those of the earlier periods, they are somewhat pretentious and flamboyant and for that reason of small interest other than for the purpose of display.

CHAPTER FOURTEEN

SALT-CELLARS

WHEN, IN THE sixteenth century, Wynkyn de Worde wrote instructions for the proper placing of the large salt—the significance of which has been described in Chapter One—and added 'at every end of ye table set a salt-seller', he introduced one of those quaint linguistic corruptions which have become part of the English language. The 'seller' or as we now spell it 'cellar' was the early English spelling of the old French *salière* (a salt-box or salt-holder) so that our prefix 'salt' is superfluous.

Our word 'salary' is another with a salty origin, though it is lost sight of to-day. It was in fact derived from the Latin *salarium* which was an allowance of salt made to soldiers and servants by the Romans; later, when money was substituted for the ration of salt, the word *salarium* was still used to denote soldiers' pay.

The 'salt-sellers' of De Worde's time and for a century and a half later, are to-day called trencher salts and so distinguished from the various styles we know as salt-cellars that appeared after about 1740.

Though we will refer to them, very few trencher salts made before the early eighteenth century exist to-day, for, being quite small, many of them would be damaged and sent to the melting pot or discarded. Those of the seventeenth century were either circular, triangular or in the form of a quatrefoil, neither shape being more than 1 inch high.

One type made toward the end of the seventeenth century was larger and somewhat more imposing. It was circular with a spreading base rather like the shape of a trumpet and ornamented on the rim and base with a wide band of spiral fluting usually referred to as gadroon. There is an example of these rare trencher salts in the Victoria and Albert Museum.

Interesting as the earlier specimens are, they lack the charm of the trencher salts made during the time of Queen Anne and

George I which have the added attraction of being still obtainable. They are invariably quite plain and either circular, oval or octagonal (Fig. 29) finely shaped and moulded. Any that come into the market to-day are usually in pairs, but on occasion a set of four or even six will come on offer.

These plain trencher salts were made for some years after the old standard of silver was restored in 1720, but they gradually went out of fashion as other styles were introduced. Their first competitor was a fairly large circular bowl which was often decorated with bold leaves on an ornamental foot. In about 1740, this gave place to the more familiar small bowl on three or four feet (Fig. 30) which has remained popular to the present time, even though it was temporarily supplanted by the various fanciful designs of the Adam style in the late eighteenth century.

There is no difficulty in finding a pair or a set of four of these later salt-cellars either almost plain or decorated. Such decoration as was applied to the plainer style is usually a gadrooned ornament round the rim and a shell form at the top of the short leg where it joins the bowl. Others which show the more pronounced influence of the French rococo are profusely ornamented with floral swags, when the shell form at the upper part of the legs is usually replaced by a lion's mask.

Another style which enjoyed a short vogue was a similar bowl on three feet but the bowl and rim were pierced with rococo scrolls, leaves and other designs and some of these have the face of a Chinaman where the leg joins the bowl. These obviously required a glass liner and this was held firm by a removable rim fitted with a bayonet fastening.

When the classic designs of Robert Adam became fashionable, the salt-cellars on three feet were superseded by the various pierced designs with glass liners and some few others of a more or less classic character. The simpler types are oval on four feet with the sides either pierced in a design of foliated scrolls with which birds are sometimes introduced or in a series of intersecting arches with vertical pillars or other geometric forms (Fig. 32). Another somewhat simpler oval type on four legs has a narrow

FIG. 29.   Octagonal trencher salt. 1725–6.   L. 3 in.

FIG. 30.   Salt-cellar of the early
rococo period. 1745–6.   H. 2¼ in.

FIG. 31.   Circular salt-cellar on
four feet.   1733–4.   H. 2 in.

FIG. 32.   Oval pierced salt-
cellar with claw and ball
feet.   1776–7.   H. 2 in.

FIG. 33.   Boat-shaped salt-
cellar. 1786–7.   H. 2½ in.

FIG. 34.   Salt-cellar and shaped
stand.   1798–9.   L. 3 in.

pierced band round the lower part, the remainder of the sides
being left solid and delicately engraved.

Other more formal styles are oval or round on a spreading
foot, both the bowl and the foot being pierced in vertical slits
with arch shapes above or in a series of intricate geometric forms.
The edges of these are decorated either with small beads or
gadroon and not infrequently festoons of leaves and other classic
ornaments are applied to the bowl.

Toward the end of the century, the fashion in salt-cellars
changed again.   The pierced work seems to have passed and the

so-called boat-shape became popular. These hold a greater
appeal to most people as they are graceful, plain and less fanciful.
Though spoken of generally as boat-shape the bowl resembles the
outline of a canoe and is raised on a stem with an oval foot.
Some of them have loop handles (Fig. 33) and are similar to the
shape of the contemporary sauce-tureens without the cover
and others finish at each end in a scroll with a ring handle.

There is one other salt-cellar of this time which if not important
is of interest as an example of the novelties which began to appear
in the last year or two of the eighteenth century. These consist
of two pieces, a bowl and a miniature dish (Fig. 34). The bowl
is shallow, but none the less suggestive of a small bowler hat
inverted and supported on a low foot, while the dish, which has
a deep well to take the foot of the bowl, is octagonal in shape with
moulded edges.

During the early nineteenth century, various so-called designs
sprang from the futile attempts to adapt earlier forms, but the
life of these often contorted shapes was brief and need not be
touched upon here. At the same time, not all the nineteenth-
century salt-cellars were of this character for there were still a
number of silversmiths who ignored the 'new designs' and were
satisfied to repeat the styles of earlier periods. And as the value
of silver of bygone days is usually in proportion to its age,
nineteenth-century copies of eighteenth-century salt-cellars make
smaller demands on the purse than the originals.

CHAPTER FIFTEEN

DREDGERS, MUFFINEERS AND CASTERS

THIS CHAPTER COULD have been titled by the one word 'Casters', as each of the articles named is used for a similar purpose, though the names themselves have different origins.

Dredger is a later form of 'drudger' which was a wooden box with a handle and holes in the top for sprinkling flour and, for that matter, still is, even if the modern ones are of metal; the word is also possibly connected with the obsolete 'dredge' which was the name of a sweatmeat containing spices. In more recent times, dredgers were made of brass with a plain cylindrical body and pierced domed slip-on cover which fitted tightly round the flange of the rim (and to-day with a modernised bayonet fastening described later in this chapter), the larger ones for sprinkling flour and the quite small ones for pepper.

Muffineer was the name of a small caster which was used to sprinkle sugar, salt or spice on muffins, while a caster formerly denoted a condiment bottle which was part of the now despised cruet-stand. In describing the various types, we propose to use the more common name caster except for the small ones with a handle, which will be referred to by their old name, dredger.

Like so many other silver articles, which came into use during the later seventeenth century, casters were introduced as a result of the always increasing amount of pepper and other spices imported to England. Pepper was known in this country during medieval times and by the time of Charles I sufficient of it was imported to attract the attention of the Treasury and a tax of 5s. a pound was imposed. That it was used on the table during the later years of Elizabeth is evident from the small pepper-caster which was part of the bell-shaped salt described in Chapter Six; and there is one in the Victoria and Albert Museum shaped like a covered cup on a foot with a pierced cap about 4 inches high which is hall-marked 1563–4.

Casters as separate articles, however, do not seem to have been

made before the reign of Charles II, when they were introduced
from France. In fact, the English casters of that time closely
resemble those which were made in France some years before.
They had a similar short cylindrical body and high top with
noticeably large piercings which would suggest they were intended for sugar or spice. And again, like the French models, the
top was fastened to the body by what is known as the bayonet
joint or fastening (Figs. 35 and 36).

This simple method of fixing a top has never been improved
upon and is used to-day even if the modern adaptations are
neater. The original bayonet joint has two slotted lugs or ears
fixed to the rim or lower outside edge of the cover from which
they project; the rim of the body has a grooved moulding in
which two notches are cut, one directly opposite the other, and
the cover is placed on so that the lugs pass the notches in the
moulding and the body is given a half turn, when it engages
firmly with the cover. Its use with modern dredgers has been
mentioned. Another good illustration of its present-day use can
be seen in an ordinary standard honey jar, the metal top of which
has four indented lugs which slip into four corresponding slots
in the moulded rim of the glass and, when given the half turn,
is 'honey-tight'.

Small cylindrical or octagonal dredgers with a simple scroll-
shaped handle appeared in the latter part of the seventeenth
century and were popular until about 1725. These delightful
little pieces are about 4 inches high and quite plain with a domical
pierced top and, even to the present time, when one is included
in a catalogue, it will be described by the romantic name 'kitchen
pepper'. Unfortunately, examples are few and far between and
when one does come up for sale it brings a fairly high price,
particularly if it is of the octagonal shape.

Early in the eighteenth century, the cylindrical caster with the
bayonet fastening gave place to the more familiar pear-shape with
a low moulded foot, of which various types were made until the
early part of George II's reign. While some of the earlier
examples of this shape have the bayonet fastening (Figs. 35 and 36)
this was soon discarded in favour of the slip-on top (Fig. 37).

FIG. 35. Pear-shaped caster with bayonet joint. 1711–12. H. 9 in.

FIG. 36. Pear-shaped caster, bayonet joint. 1708–9. H. 8 in.

FIG. 37. Caster made in Exeter. 1720. H. 6 in.

FIG. 38. Caster made by Paul De Lamerie. 1738–9. H. 7 in.

During the early Georgian period, an appreciable number of
casters were made eight sided (Fig. 35) doubtless to achieve a
sense of light and shade and so relieve the somewhat severe outline of the plain pear-shape (Fig. 36). Apart from this, the
casters generally depend for their ornamentation upon the finely
pierced tops. The tops are quite high, in fact about half the
height of the body, and are shaped to continue the outline of the
narrow end of the pear. They are, as a rule, divided into vertical
panels each of which is delicately pierced with tiny shapes; but
in some the top is divided by a small horizontal band when the
piercing is of an entirely different character (compare Figs. 35
and 37 with Fig. 36).

In most instances the eighteenth-century pear-shaped casters
have the bulbous part below (Fig. 36), but they were also made
with the bulbous part above (Fig. 37). In the larger number,
however, the body is in two parts, the lower being the wider
rounded section of the pear and the upper the tapered 'waist' and
the outline is completed by the tall domical pierced top. This
style of caster has a moulded band round the joint of the two
sections; and in some cases, has the effect of a distinct shoulder
which breaks the pear outline (Fig. 38).

Casters of the types described were commonly made in sets of
three, and though over the years some of them become separated,
a number of complete sets exist to the present time (each of those
illustrated is one of a complete set). They consist of one large
caster, sometimes 9 inches high for sugar or salt and two smaller
ones for Jamaica and Cayenne pepper or, as they are better known
to-day, black and red pepper.

In the later rococo period, the lower rounded section of the
pear assumed the wavy-curve outline, referred to in previous
chapters, and the former high domed top also takes a wavy shape
and tapers. Like the preceding type, the body is divided by a
moulded band into two parts though the lower is wider in
proportion to the upper section. This shape is often referred to
as vase-shape and sometimes as the inverted pyriform.

Several varieties were made during the Adam period, including
a number with pierced sides, sometimes decorated with classic

ornaments; these were fitted with glass liners and most of them are rather insignificant little specimens and of little interest except for use on a breakfast tray (Fig. 39).

At this time, there was a revival of the cylindrical shape with the bayonet joint, described above; but the top instead of being pierced with the quatrefoils and similar forms of the earlier period, was pierced with vertical slits and arches ornamented

FIG. 39. Late Georgian caster. 1794-5. H. $3\frac{1}{4}$ in.

FIG. 40. Pierced mustard-pot. 1790-1. H. $2\frac{1}{4}$ in.

with festoons; a large number were also made of glass fitted with pierced tops, but these were intended for the now almost forgotten cruet-stands.

Cruet-stands or cruet-frames, to use the correct term, of the type known as the Warwick which were fashionable about the middle of the eighteenth century, were fitted with one large and two small casters of silver, usually pear-shape, and two cut-glass cruets with silver caps. Warwick cruet-frames still exist complete, but it is fairly safe to say that many were 'dismantled' when they went out of date and the set of three silver casters preserved. The various casters and cruets of the late eighteenth- and early nineteenth-century frames were of glass with silver tops; and some of the frames are a veritable *multum in parvo* for they include a pepper caster, a sugar caster, two large oil and vinegar bottles with silver neck mount and handle, two other small bottles and a mustard-pot.

The addition of a mustard-pot to the cruet was a late eighteenth-century innovation, because previously they were invariably

separate articles. Mustard was known and used at least by early
Tudor times as is evident from Shakespeare's *Taming of the Shrew*
where Grumio teases the hungry Katharina and suggests 'a piece
of beef and mustard'. It seems probable that at that time the
finely ground powder was sprinkled on the meat and not mixed
with water to form a paste until about a century later. Incidentally, mustard was made by grinding the seed of the freely growing plant we know by that name, and mixing it with the unfer-
mented juice of grapes which was called must.

Though there is evidence that silver mustard-pots were made
in the time of Charles II, the earliest existing examples date from
the early Georgian times, and those are extremely rare. In fact,
it would appear almost that they did not come into general use
until the second half of the eighteenth century when a variety
of shapes and styles were produced; specimens of the late Georgian
period are fairly plentiful.

Most of them are drum-shape or oval and all of them are
attractive pieces of silverwork. Some are pierced with geometric
or other designs (Fig. 40) but both shapes were also made plain.
All of them, whether pierced or plain, are fitted with glass liners,
because mustard causes silver to tarnish quickly as is evident when
a silver spoon is used for mustard.

During the early nineteenth century, the pierced sides went out
of fashion and one style of mustard-pot which was made at that
time is reminiscent of the seventeenth-century drum-shaped
tankard, for the makers even repeated the shape of the tankard
lid and the thumb-piece.

CHAPTER SIXTEEN

BASKETS AND EPERGNES

OF ALL THE numerous forms of ornamentation with English and Irish silverwork, none shows more refinement and skill than the pierced designs of the baskets, epergnes and other articles. Baskets for bread or cake were made in the time of Charles II, but surviving examples are too rare to be of interest here, except in so far as they may be said to be the models of those which became fashionable later.

With few exceptions, the eighteenth-century baskets are oval and the first style which appeared in the reign of George II was pierced and chased to suggest wicker-work. These have a loop handle at each end instead of the later and more familiar swing or, as it is called, bale handle which was adopted about 1740 when baskets for bread, cake, fruit and sweetmeats became part of the table silver in all larger houses.

All the pierced designs before the later eighteenth century are exceptionally elegant without being in any way extravagant. As might be expected in view of their having been introduced by the Huguenot silversmiths, they show a pronounced rococo influence, which is particularly evident in the scroll-work, masks, shells, cherubs' heads, lions' masks and other cast ornaments applied as a border.

The silversmiths evolved especially intricate and diverse arrangements yet never failed to preserve a perfect balance and symmetry. Small pierced foliated scrolls were arranged to form, as it were, a background for panels of tiny crosses (Fig. 41); or the whole of the sides would be pierced with different shaped panels of diapers (repetition of some small geometrical shapes), scrolls, quatrefoils, enclosed by chased bands of beads; in other instances the design would consist of foliage, fruit, flowers, sheaves of corn in C-scroll-shaped panels, in addition to many other attractive combinations.

There is a similar diversity with the swing handles which vary

FIG. 41. Basket with handle, pierced and decorated in the rococo style. 1742–3. L. 14½ in.

from the elaborate style formed of two terminal figures supporting an arch decorated with flowers and scrolls in relief to the plain
bow type and the lighter handle of cabled wire—the last mentioned lacks the beauty of the other stouter styles.

In the last quarter of the eighteenth century, the pierced work
came under the influence of the classic designs and is unquestion-
ably less attractive than that of the earlier styles described above.
The pierced patterns were formal and would, for example, consist of a combination of scrolls, small arches and guilloche,
vitruvian or other classic meanders; the guilloche ornament is
intertwining bands or lines arranged so as to leave a circular or
oval opening and the vitruvian a series of scrolls shaped rather
like the Chinese symbols for waves, and both were borrowed
from classic architecture.

One 'short-cut' method of producing a pierced effect which
was practiced in the second half of the eighteenth century was to
make a basket shape of silver wire—not unlike a lamp shade

inverted, but with more ribs—and apply flowers, leaves and other ornaments which had been hammered up from thin silver. This was possibly copied from similar work that was made in France, but the baskets made in this way are almost tawdry when compared with the fine examples which were hammered up or raised, as it is technically known, from sheet silver and then carefully pierced. And we may admire the skill of the men who produced those baskets, for any deviation of the tool might mean that the design was irretrievably spoiled.

Another type of cake-basket which was popular about the middle of the eighteenth century was made in the form of a large deep shell with a cast scroll handle in the shape of a female bust and raised on three dolphin feet. Part of the basket was ribbed to resemble an escallop shell and the remainder variously pierced. But though these are interesting and desirable possessions, the likelihood of one becoming available is, to say the least, somewhat remote.

Many of the baskets made during the early nineteenth century lack the dignified beauty of the earlier examples. For the most part, they give the impression of having been made as cheaply as possible. Some of them are without any pierced work but merely a shape with a shell and gadroon border and a quite plain handle; and even when they are pierced, this is limited to a narrow band of slits or some equally unattractive design round the rim and possibly round the foot—certainly none of them inspires any admiration of the design or the workmanship.

We have previously referred to the massive centrepieces or epergnes which were fashionable in the early part of the rococo period. After about 1750 these were largely replaced by a lighter style with a taller frame fitted with a pierced centre dish and smaller dishes and baskets for fruit and sweetmeats.

These later epergnes are often quite elaborate but never fanciful, though the ornamentation is essentially rococo. The stand or frame is raised on four scroll legs with shell feet, a large basket rests on top of the stand and scroll brackets fitted into the legs extend outward to support smaller baskets with swing handles and circular dishes. The larger epergnes have as many as four little baskets and four dishes, but examples of this size would occupy a considerable space on a table, for the overall 'spread' is 24 inches or possibly more.

Some epergnes of this time show the Chinese influence in the use of a pagoda shaped canopy, or, at times, two canopies with eight small pendant bells. The canopies are supported on four light pillars which rest on a pierced base with rococo legs and feet. A large basket for fruit is set between the pillars, and brackets with baskets and dishes are fitted as described above.

Epergnes of the early nineteenth century, which were strongly influenced by the French Empire style, are cumbersome, ostentatious objects fitted with glass dishes and without interest except to illustrate the ugly forms which at that time paraded as design.

CHAPTER SEVENTEEN

CANDLESTICKS AND CANDELABRA

WHEN PRIMITIVE MAN decided he would like to have some light to cheer the hours of darkness, he bound strips of bark or wood together, dipped them in tallow and so invented the candle. And there are references to splinters of 'fatted' wood having been used by the humbler classes in England six centuries ago. Wax candles were known in this country during the Middle Ages, but, owing to their high cost, their use was restricted to religious and ceremonial purposes. And though wax became cheaper in the fifteenth century, the 'tallow dip' as it was popularly known continued to be made for domestic use until relatively modern times.

Wax candles, however, were used in larger houses from that time on and this is illustrated by the fact that the makers of wax candles were then distinguished from those who made tallow candles, as both the Wax Chandlers' Company and the Tallow Chandlers' Company were incorporated in the later years of the fifteenth century.

Candlesticks of precious metals are mentioned frequently in the Old Testament and were doubtless made in quite early times in Britain. For our present interest, we may begin the story when William and Mary replaced James II, because very few silver candlesticks made before that time would offer much attraction in a modern house—even if they were obtainable. Those which have survived are mostly museum curiosities.

Therefore, the first style we need concern ourselves with is that with the columnar shaft presumably copied from the Greek Doric architectural column which became fashionable in the last quarter of the seventeenth century and is equally popular at the present time. They are upward of 11 inches high with a wide octagonal or square moulded base and were made in pairs and sets of four though the sets are not easy to find.

But the vogue for these columnar candlesticks was short-lived and by the end of the century they gave place to the cast type with the baluster stem. This almost sudden change was probably due to the fact that a cast candlestick can be made more easily than the columnar shaft, and is, moreover, much stronger and therefore less likely to be damaged.

In casting candlesticks, the usual practice was to prepare a model in wax from which a mould was made. The silver, which was heated to a liquefied state, was poured into the mould and, when cold, the candlestick was cleaned and finished; ornaments such as were adopted during the rococo period were cast separately and soldered on.

Baluster candlesticks of the high standard period are mostly quite plain, any decoration that was used being restricted to gadrooning round the base, the knop and the socket. And the baluster stems of the first cast candlesticks are especially interesting because the shape of the shaft or stem when studied shows a noticeable resemblance to a drinking cup. As a rule, the foot, that is the section joining the stem to the base, is concave and widens downward to a saucer-like well in an octagonal moulded base. The last sentence may sound rather technical, but it describes the more outstanding features which are illustrated in Fig. 42.

Within a few years, the complete cup-shape disappeared but a relic of it remained in a bulbous knop or shoulder at the top of the stem (Fig. 43); the section which was formerly the 'foot' of the cup-shape was lengthened to a plain or faceted taper resting on a smaller bulbous knop; and with the octagonal or hexagonal (faceted) stem the former low base was replaced by a high foot and moulded base of the same outline as the stem (Fig. 44).

After about 1735 until the classic designs became fashionable in the later eighteenth century, a wide variety of stems and bases were used with candlesticks; and while these are fundamentally of the baluster type, the outline of the shape is often lost beneath the applied ornamental forms which were introduced by Paul De Lamerie and his fellow Huguenot silversmiths (Fig. 45).

FIG. 42. Plain bal-
uster candlestick.
1702–3. H. 6½ in.

FIG. 43. Candlestick
with decorated base.
1749–50. H. 8 in.

FIG. 44. Candlestick
with faceted knop.
1706–7. H. 6¾ in.

FIG. 45. Candlestick
in the rococo style.
1754–5. H. 9 in.

FIG. 46. Candlestick
on square base.
1771–2. H. 7½ in.

FIG. 47. Decor-
ated candlestick.
1773–4. H. 9 in.

But if many of the candlesticks of this period are of the florid
rococo style, there is no scarcity of others which are far less
ornate and of a character appropriate in any modern setting.
These plainer types depend for their ornamentation upon the
shaping of the baluster stem and similar shaping of the moulded
bases. Some of them have shell forms on the shoulder of
the stem and similar but larger shells on the base (Fig. 43)

and there are various other simple but attractive styles (Figs. 46 and 47).

By about 1765, there was a complete change in the styles of candlesticks and the baluster stem and all other rococo forms gave place to the various columnar types inspired by the ancient architecture discovered at Herculaneum and Pompeii. The candlesticks which were intended for the interiors designed by Robert Adam were ornamented with rams' and lions' heads, festoons and other essentially classic forms; but such candlesticks as these hold less appeal for most of us than the simpler columnar shafts (Fig. 48). Most of the latter more or less faithfully follow the Corinthian order of architecture, 'more or less' because, as Mr. Frederick Bradbury remarked, 'the designers deviated freely from the severe purity of the source of their inspiration and introduced many alien details'. But even if the silversmiths did sometimes use an Ionic capital with a Corinthian column or produced a shaft of clustered columns (Fig. 49) which has no architectural prototype, the candlesticks are no less handsome.

Other somewhat later types have a four-sided shaft tapering downward to a square base or a fluted round shaft tapering to a circular base, each of which has a classic vase-shaped socket. These and other late eighteenth-century designs continued to be made during the early years of the nineteenth century.

There is no need to touch at length upon candelabra (Fig. 50) as they are merely candlesticks fitted with two or more branches; it is worth noting, however, that as candelabra may be used as candlesticks by removing the branches, so any suitable candlestick will serve as a base for branches. And it is not uncommon to find that the branches of a candelabrum are of a later date than the stick to which they are fitted.

Snuffers with their accompanying little tray or in a stand were formerly indispensable requisites to candlesticks and still hold a certain romantic appeal even if they are unnecessary in our time. With present-day candles, the wick is consumed at the same rate as the wax, but time was when it was necessary to clip the wick at intervals to prevent its causing the wax or tallow to run down the candle. The snuffers are similar to a pair of scissors, one blade

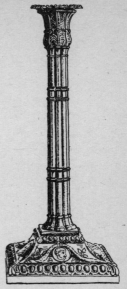

FIG. 49. Columnar candlestick on square base. 1774-5. H. 12½ in.

FIG. 48. Columnar candlestick of the Adam period. 1775-6. H. 14 in.

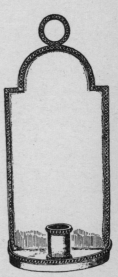

FIG. 50. Plain candelabrum with square pear-shaped stem and octagonal faceted plinth. 1712-13. H. 8¾ in.

FIG. 51. Plain wall sconce with gadrooned borders. 1810-11. H. 11½ in.

being fitted with a small box and the other with a plate, and, when used, the latter pinches off the superfluous part of the wick and presses it into the box.

Wall sconces (Fig. 51) and the small portable or, as it is called, bedroom candlestick are other relics of the days when electric light was unknown and man's inventions were not controlling the inventors.

CHAPTER EIGHTEEN

PLATES AND DISHES

As LATE AS the time of Charles II, wooden trenchers which were the forerunners of the dinner plate, were still used even at banquets. Pepys writing of a banquet he attended at the Guildhall complained that 'None . . . but the Mayors and Lords of the Privy Council had napkins or knives which was very strange. . . . It was very unpleasing that we had no napkins nor change of trenchers and drunk out of earthen and wood bowls.' A later entry of another dinner at which he was a guest expressed his pleasure at 'eating in silver dishes and all things mighty rich and handsome about me'.

The trenchers mentioned by Pepys were possibly the flat square piece of wood which took the place of the earlier thick slices of bread, or they may have been the more advanced circular shape with the shallow well and narrow flat rim.

And though we could assume that the average home of the late Georgian period would have porcelain and the more wealthy silver plates and dishes, pewter services and wooden trenchers were still in fairly common use at least as late as the first quarter of the nineteenth century. Presumably, the more expensive porcelain and silver were reserved for special occasions, for a magazine of 1822 mentions that the more wealthy families had a service of pewter 'but amongst the middling and poorer classes the dinner was eaten off wooden trenchers'.

These wooden trenchers were the circular ones about 9 inches diameter of sycamore wood turned on the lathe. The shape was, in fact, copied both by the silversmith and the potter, so that, though the name has been changed to 'plate', we still eat from a 'trencher', a word the English language borrowed from the Old French *trenchier* (to cut); and it still survives in the name of the round piece of wood on which bread is cut, known as a bread trencher, also, until fairly recent times, in 'butter trencher' which was a smaller piece of wood in the bottom of a butter-dish.

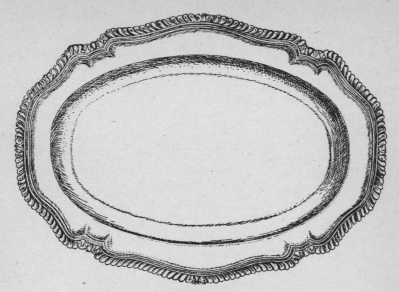

FIG. 52. Large shaped meat dish with gadroon
and leaf ornamental border. 1744–5. L. 20 in.

FIG. 53. Entrée dish, the cover fitted with
detachable handle. 1813–14. L. 11 in.

Actually, the principal difference between the wooden and the
more expensive 'trenchers' of our time is the decoration of the
latter, the silver ones often having a shaped rim with a gadrooned
(Fig. 52) or other ornamental border while those of porcelain
are finely painted with floral and various other subjects.

Dishes with covers of the kind we know as entree dishes were
added to the table silver in the late eighteenth century. For the

larger services, they were made in sets of four, six or even more, either round, octagonal or oval with a gadrooned or other ornament on the rim and the top of the cover to match the other pieces.

Most of them are about 10 inches long and have a flat cover

FIG. 54.   Entrée dish with high cover
and hot-water base.   1811–12.   L. 12 in.

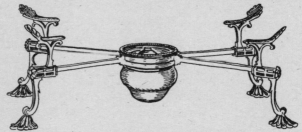

FIG. 55.   Dish-cross with adjustable
arms and brackets.   1775–6.   L. 12 in.

fitted with a detachable handle which allows the cover to be used as a separate dish if required (Fig. 53), but some of the larger ones are upward of 15 inches long and these often have an extra base, usually of Sheffield plate, for hot water to keep the contents of the entrée dish hot (Fig. 54).   Other shallower dishes with covers, such as could be used for bacon or savouries, are fitted with an interior lining and a long turned wood handle; this handle is made to screw into the socket through which hot water was poured into the space underneath the dish and the handle then being replaced.

These always useful dishes have never gone out of fashion and while new styles were produced during the early nineteenth century and since, the original type with the detachable handle has continued popular; and most of the other types are equally attractive and as useful, even though those with domical covers cannot be used as two separate dishes.

One, now almost forgotten, method of keeping food hot in bygone days was an ingenious contrivance, known as a dish-cross (Fig. 55) which also came into use during the time of George III. It consists of two rings, one above the other. Two arms or rods are fixed to each ring so that the arms may be opened or closed according to the *width* of the dish—actually much on the same principle as a pair of scissors. Each arm is fitted with a bracket attached to a supporting foot, the brackets being made to slide along the arms to accommodate the *length* of the dish. When the arms are spread wide and the brackets adjusted, a dish-cross will support a large venison dish; or by bringing the arms closer together and the brackets toward the centre, it can be used to hold a small saucepan, the heat being furnished by a spirit lamp under the rings in which there is a perforated disk.

CHAPTER NINETEEN

SAUCE-BOATS, SAUCE-TUREENS AND ARGYLES

IT IS DOUBTFUL whether we moderns see any resemblance to a boat or ship in the graceful little sauce-boats which are familiar to us to-day; but, actually they are descendants of an earlier shape which has an unmistakable similarity to the outline of an ancient ship. The silversmiths possibly developed this shape from the massive silver table ornament of medieval times known as a nef, which was a complete model of a sailing ship—the nef was reserved for the use of kings and nobles and is believed to have held a knife, spoon and various other articles including a piece of narwhal's tusk which, when mixed with wine, was supposed to show if some unfriendly person had added a dose of poison.

Sauce-boats, when they first came into use in England in the early eighteenth century, were boat-shape with a high prow-like lip at each end and either a bale handle across the middle of the 'hull' or a loop handle on each side to allow passing along the table (see Fig. 77). As a rule, they have a moulded foot, but some of them have four legs and, though examples of either are by no means plentiful, they are obtainable.

It is possible to imagine that minor disasters could occur at the dinner table, and the sauce spilled, if one of these earlier sauce-boats were not handled carefully. And it was probably for this reason that they were discarded in favour of the single-lipped shape with a stout handle.

Except for the many fanciful shapes produced by some of the Huguenot silversmiths during the rococo period, which do not concern us here, the shape adopted in the time of George I has, to all intents, remained unchanged. At first, the bowl was raised on a moulded foot, but within a short time this was replaced by the more attractive three short legs usually with hoof or shell feet.

Some of the bowls are embossed and chased with scrolls, flowers, shellwork and similar rococo ornaments and these often have feet of the scroll type (Fig. 56) or in the form of lions' paws and a lion's mask where the upper part of the leg joins the bowl. Most of them, however, are plain, apart from a finely modelled

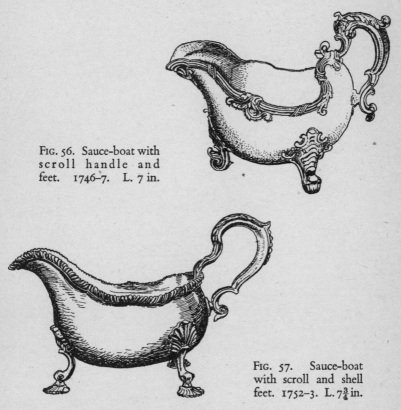

FIG. 56. Sauce-boat with scroll handle and feet. 1746–7.   L. 7 in.

FIG. 57.   Sauce-boat with scroll and shell feet. 1752–3.   L. 7¾ in.

handle, which is usually the double scroll shape, and a shell at the upper part of the legs (Fig. 57).

During the earlier Georgian period, the edge of the bowl was cut in a series of undulating curves, often of what is known as the double cyma shape (⌒‿⌒) without any applied ornament, but after about 1750, the edge was generally gadrooned (Fig. 57). Sauce-boats of a similar shape to those described, were made during the reign of George III, but they were, to a great extent, superseded by the small turcens with covers, which were made in pairs or sets of four.

For practical purposes, there are two styles of these tureens, one of which has a small handle at each end (Fig. 58), and the other is boat-shaped with high looped handles on a concave foot with

FIG. 58.   Late Georgian sauce-tureen.   1805–6.   L. 8 in.

FIG. 59.   Boat-shaped sauce-tureen.   1790–1.   L. 9 in.

a plinth (Fig. 59).   The first are sometimes decorated in a manner indicating a carry-over of the rococo influence to the Adam period, an influence that shows itself in such ornaments as foliated scrolls, bold lions' masks, and scroll feet.   Some of these are accompanied by a shaped silver dish or stand either separate or fixed to the feet—with the fixed stand they are by no means easy to clean properly and for this reason were never popular.

Those who admire graceful line rather than elaborate orna-mentation would doubtless prefer the boat-shaped tureens of the Adam style (Fig. 59).   While some of these are decorated with garlands, medallions and other classic forms, most of them are plain or perhaps have a simple gadrooned rim and some delicately chased leaf ornament on the domical cover, but there is no applied ornament to break the rhythmic curve of the body.

Both styles of the sauce-tureens illustrated in Figs. 58 and 59 continued to be made during the nineteenth century; and those of the early years repeat the rococo ornamentation with admirable restraint and faithfully reproduce the fine lines of the classic boat-shape.

Another vessel which made its appearance on the dinner table during the time of George III and which might be called a companion to the sauce-tureen is known as an argyle—though it is fairly safe to say that few except those who have given some study to old silver would recognize one.

Actually it is an ingenious gravy holder which was invented by someone, traditionally named Argyle, who objected to cold gravy. We all object to it, but our friend discovered a means to prevent its becoming cold and his invention was widely popular during the last quarter of the eighteenth and the early part of the nineteenth century, when every well-equipped table was furnished with at least one argyle.

They are usually similar to a small straight-sided tea-pot with a straight tubular spout or a vase-shaped coffee-pot with a curved

Fig. 60.   Argyle or gravy-holder with hot-water compartment.   1798-9.   H. 7 in.

spout.   A socket with a small cover was fixed in the middle of the pot and a billet of heated iron was placed in the socket to keep the gravy hot—it could be described as a piece of hot iron surrounded by gravy (see Fig. 60).

Recognizing this method was cumbersome, it was not long before the silversmiths evolved a simpler means of heating the gravy with hot water.   Later argyles were therefore fitted with an inner lining or jacket into which the water was poured through a small spout with a hinged flap.   This type has a swan-neck spout set low down the side of the body, where it passes through the hot water jacket to the inside chamber which holds the gravy; with these, the handle is at right angles to the spout which is of considerable convenience when pouring.

Various uses to which argyles can be put in our time have been mentioned in an earlier chapter.

CHAPTER TWENTY

SALVERS AND TRAYS

MUCH OF INTEREST is to be found in the names of things in everyday use, as for example salvers or waiters, as they are also known, and trays, each of which has a curious and not un-romantic derivation; and strictly speaking a different meaning, though in modern times they are more or less interchangeable.

Salver comes from the Spanish *salvar*—to taste and prove food or drink before serving it. In time, it came to denote the flat plate on which things were presented by a servant; the smaller ones are commonly known as card trays though the name salver or waiter still denotes the larger ones.

To suggest that the word 'waiter' is connected with the Yule-tide serenaders we know as waits might seem fanciful, but actually it derived from the same source. The antiquary Rymer in his curious account of the duties and rewards of the 'waytes' refers to the circumstances under which a wait might become a 'groome watere' who was a kind of page or personal servant or the 'yeoman-waiter' of slightly later; subsequently, the word was applied to a man who attended at the dinner table and also to the dish or tray on which he carried food and other articles.

There are several, now obsolete, names which were formerly applied to different servants who attended at the 'borde' or dinner table, as we know it: For example, the man who carried in the joint on a large dish called a charger was also known as the charger; similarly, the one who carved it was the trencher; and the menial who gathered up the fragments after a meal was the voider, the 'leavings' being collected into a large tray or basket, known as a voider with a voiding-knife—doubtless the ancestors of the crumb-scoop and tray beloved of the Victorian era.

When tea services came into fashion in the time of George III, the name tray seems to have been adopted for the large oval and rectangular trays on which the service was placed to distinguish them from the circular and square salvers. The word came from the Anglo-Saxon *treg* or *trig* which still survives in country districts in the word 'trug' meaning the long shallow trough-like basket made of wide strips of wood used by gardeners.

Silver salvers came into use in England during the time of Charles II when, as they are described by a contemporary writer, they were 'broad and flat with a foot underneath'. At the end of the seventeenth century the top was made smaller but the foot,

FIG. 61.   Salver engraved in the rococo style.   1758-9.   15¾ in. sq.

which was trumpet-shape, remained, the salver being held by the foot when presenting anything on it. The smaller circular salver on a foot continued to be made during the first few years of the eighteenth century and, incidentally, is often referred to as a tazza.

Within a short time, however, these gave place to the more attractive shapes on three or four short feet of which a large variety of designs were made during the days of the early Georgian kings. One of the first shapes to appear was square or oblong with indented corners and a plain moulded border, the surface of the salver being either plain or engraved with a narrow band of rococo decoration (Figs. 61 and 62).

FIG. 62.   Oblong tray engraved with narrow band
of diaper, masks, shells, etc.   1726–7.   L. 18 in.

Others were octagonal but the larger number were circular,
the outline of which was varied by the use of incurves and small
angles with rounded corners, or by a series of convex and concave
curves, or the use of scrolls to vary the plain outline of the circle
(Fig. 63).   Others were shaped by a series of curves known
technically as multifoil, illustrated in Fig. 64.

Ornate borders, before the Adam style became fashionable,
were mostly composed of characteristically rococo forms such as
gadrooning, shells and scrolls.   On the smaller salvers the
ornamentation was not extravagant, but with some of the larger
circular examples, which are upward of 24 inches in diameter it
was often unduly massive.   It is also noticeable that the decoration of the surface of the tray became more profuse as time went
on.   At first, it was restricted to a narrow band as described
above, but the band later became wider and wider until almost
the entire surface was covered.

Immediately before the full blossoming of the Adam style,
some salvers were made which show in their decoration what

FIG. 63.   Tray decorated with engraving and
scroll and shell border.   1745–6.   D. 22 in.

might be termed the transition from the rococo to the classic.
Like others of the later eighteenth century, these are circular and
the ornamental border shows the waning rococo in the use of
small scrolls and shells and the coming of the classic styles in
festoons, rosettes and similar forms typical of the Adam period.

Others, slightly later, are oval or octagonal, the borders being
pierced and chased with different classic forms such as rams'
heads, husks, drapery and a beaded or reeded edge.   The beaded
edge was also used with the quite plain circular salvers, but one
would hesitate to suggest that these are impressive.

During the early part of the nineteenth century, the pierced
border remained popular, though by then the designs are often
somewhat coarse. Generally speaking however, the salvers
which followed the Adam style are faithful copies of the circular
type fashionable during the rococo period.

FIG. 64. Scalloped or multifoil tray with gadrooned border. 1724-5. W. 20 in.

Complete tea and coffee services did not come into general use until the reign of George III at which time the larger oval and other shaped trays were made. But before the middle of the eighteenth century, large circular and other trays (Fig. 63) were used to hold the various articles comprising what was called the 'tea equipage'. The tray of that time was known as the 'tea table' and was supported on a mahogany stand with sockets cut in the top to take the feet of the tray and hold it firmly; the top of the stand was the same size as the tray it was intended for and they are referred to in early Georgian records as 'stands to set the silver Tea and Coffee Tables on'.

Tea-trays of the Adam period were often oval with a pierced silver gallery (Fig. 65), hand-holes, and either a silver, wood or papier mâché bottom, but though convenient from the point of being light, the style attained no lasting popularity. After the

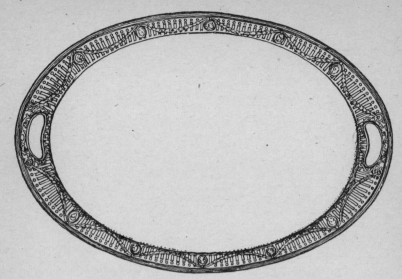

FIG. 65.   Plain oval tray with pierced rim of
the late Georgian period. 1816–17.   L. 26 in.

FIG. 66.   Oval tray of the late Georgian period
with rococo ornaments.   1807–8.   L. 27 in.

passing of the classic vogue at the end of the eighteenth century,
there was a reversion to the rococo forms of decoration with the
large oval trays as with the circular salver.   It is not difficult to

find plain examples with a shell and gadrooned border (Fig. 66) and these nineteenth-century trays are of a character which proves that, where they were content to copy and not 'adapt', the silversmiths of that time produced work equal to that of any other period.

CHAPTER TWENTY-ONE

STANDISHES AND INKSTANDS

MANY OLD-TIME GRACES have been sacrificed to our modern hurried way of life and one of them is illustrated in our manner of treating private correspondence. To-day, we are quite apt to disregard the courtesy of sending a short note to acknowledge a favour or to express the pleasure enjoyed during a stay with a friend—if perchance we are alive to the obligation, it is more likely to be fulfilled via the ubiquitous telephone or written on a typewriter.

Here a story apropos correspondence and courtesy: One of those charming old planters whom one meets in the Southern United States became acquainted with a man from New England who was visiting the South. When the latter had returned home, he received a letter from his new friend expressing the pleasure he had enjoyed from the meeting. The envelope contained two letters, one of which was written on the typewriter and explained, 'Out of courtesy to you, I write in my own hand, but to save your time and spare you the annoyance of deciphering it, I also send a typewritten copy which I have had prepared for you'.

Time was, before the early sixteenth century, when writing was done by travelling clerks who with their inkhorn, sand-caster, quills and a knife for sharpening the quills went from place to place inscribing letters and records for their betters. When, however, writing came to be numbered among the social graces, these itinerant scribes, lacking adequate employment, started to write the news of the day; and their 'news sheets' were sold to those who could afford them or read to a group of people in return for a 'collection'.

Writing a letter in bygone days could not be hurried. There were no fountain pens, blotting paper or gummed envelopes. The standish or, as we now call it, inkstand was equipped with an inkpot with a series of holes in the top to take the quill pens when not in use, or a separate pen-pot, another with a perforated top

FIG. 67.   Standish or inkstand with sand-
caster, bell and ink-pot.   1705-6.   L. 11½ in.

for sprinkling fine sand on the paper to dry the ink and in many
instances, a bell to summon a servant (Fig. 67).

While English silver inkstands of the seventeenth century do
exist, they are too few to be of interest here.   In fact it was not
until the beginning of the eighteenth century that they seem to
have come into general use, and at that time and for many years
afterwards, they rank with the finest examples of plainer English
silverwork.

Many were made by one or another of the Huguenot silversmiths and while a few of these are extravagantly decorated, as
for example, one belonging to the Goldsmiths' Company which
was made by Paul De Lamerie, most of them are entirely free of
ornamentation, except perhaps for a gadrooned edge to the dish.
The dishes vary in shape and in some instances the sides were
raised thus giving the effect of a shallow oval basin with a flat
bottom as the one shown in Fig. 67; they vary also in size from
about 9 inches to 15 inches long.

Inkstands of the later eighteenth century differ little in the
matter of their equipment from the earlier ones, but cut-glass pots
with silver tops were used instead of the former silver ones.
The dishes or stands of many are quite similar to those of the
preceding period and in some instances the glass pots are fitted

in plain silver sockets, and with others the sockets are pierced. These and other styles, among them the fine casket inkstands with the double lid hinged in the centre, continued to be made well into the nineteenth century.

One of the several requisites to the writing table in other days was a taper holder for a miniature candle to melt the sealing wax. Occasionally, one of these little tapersticks, as they are called, was included with the fitments of an inkstand; but, as a general rule, one or a pair of separate taper-holders similar in style to the contemporary candlesticks was on the writing desk.

Another kind of taper-holder, generally called a wax-jack or wax-winder was also used, though any specimens of silver are now very rare. With these a flexible wax taper was wound round a horizontal spindle fitted in a frame with a tray; the end of the taper passed through a hole in a disk at the top and a small conical extinguisher was attached by a chain to the frame.

Where an inkstand is equipped with a bell or a taper-holder it often covers a small receptacle to hold wafers, but here again, a separate wafer-box was more usual. Wafers were small disks of dried paste used to fasten letters before envelopes were invented.

Envelopes of the kind familiar to-day did not come into general use until about 1850. A type of envelope was known some years earlier and it was these which Rowland Hill referred to as 'little bags called envelopes'. In 1840, when the penny post was intro-duced, William Mulready, the artist, designed a postal envelope decorated with allegorical subjects, but the public refused to accept them and most of them were destroyed. Four years later two machines for making envelopes were patented.

Steel pens had almost entirely replaced the quill by the time envelopes were in general use, while blotting paper began to replace the sand-caster in about 1830.

CHAPTER TWENTY-TWO

SOUVENIRS OF OLD-TIME CUSTOMS

IN THIS CHAPTER, we will turn from the more practical to the romantic and speak of small pieces of early silverwork which are associated with the customs of bygone generations. For, if as time passed and fashion changed many of these articles went out of use, a few have been and more can be revived to serve other purposes, some of which have been suggested in an earlier chapter. And with their new usefulness they combine something of the romance of those days when, as the old ballad has it, 'Things were sure if a trifle slow, but the world went very well then'.

COASTERS

When, in the late eighteenth century, it became fashionable to remove the cloth after the table was cleared for dessert, the polished mahogany top was very liable to damage from the decanter being pushed along the top. Then some ingenious mind conceived the idea of placing the decanter in a circular stand with fairly deep sides of silver and a wood base covered underneath with baize. The baize prevented the table top from being scratched when the decanter and stand were pushed or 'coasted' along from one to the other; and it is not difficult to imagine that often as the evening wore on, the coasting was slightly erratic.

They were often made in pairs and mounted on a miniature cart with two or four silver wheels; and there are examples of the early nineteenth century in the form of a barge or boat mounted on a chassis with four wheels rather similar to that of a child's miniature perambulator. These wheeled coasters were sometimes referred to as wine-wagons and Frederick Bradbury suggests they were evolved by Sir E. Thomason of Birmingham; but at the same time, Mr. Bradbury notes that 'wine-wagons are to be met with in both silver and Sheffield plate apparently made late in the eighteenth century'.

For a time during the early nineteenth century both the simple circular plain and the pierced styles continued to be made, but these were superseded by various shapes embossed with different patterns which in most instances have relatively little to recommend them.

PAP-BOATS

Different lexicographers suggest different sources from which we derived the curious word 'pap', but they agree that it originated from the sound which an infant makes when calling for food or in feeding. Thus it came to be applied to semi-liquid and soft food such as is given to infants and invalids.

Pap-boats are small shallow vessels about 4 inches long and

FIG. 68.   Pap-boat.
1764-5.   L. 4½ in.

similar in shape to a sauce-boat with a similarly long wide lip which is particularly convenient in feeding those who are too weak to feed themselves. In fact the same method is used to the present time though the pap-boat is of white porcelain, but about the same size as the silver ones. It should be pointed out, however, that a pap-boat is always without a foot and very rarely has a handle (Fig. 68).

They were made of silver in the seventeenth century and possibly before as the word 'pap' occurs in the title of one of the famous Marprelate tracts which were published in 1589 by John Penry or Ap-Henry, the Welsh Puritan; and the title, *Pap with a Hatchet* gave rise to the old adage 'He gives pap with a hatchet' to denote doing a kindness grudgingly and rudely. The phrase occurs in *Discourse of Marriage and Wiving* which warns that 'He that so old seeks for a Nurse so young, shall have Pap with a Hatchet for his Comfort'.

SAUCEPANS

It is probable that most of us would regard our hostess as amusingly eccentric if, at a dinner party, food was brought to the dining-room in a saucepan, even if it were a silver one. Yet this method of serving hot foods was still fashionable less than a century ago, because, formerly, the kitchen was often some considerable distance from the dining-room.

There is no doubt that the custom dates from quite ancient

FIG. 69. Ogee-shaped saucepan with lip
and wood handle. 1819-20. H. 5 in.

times, because similar saucepan-like vessels of the Roman period have been unearthed in Britain and examples of these are in the British Museum. The two earliest English saucepan-like objects of silver that have come to the writer's notice are both rather clumsy objects of the skillet type with a stout handle; one made in Cromwell's time has three stumpy pear-shaped legs but is without a cover and the other, made in 1665, has legs with claw feet and a cover with a flat pierced handle at the side.

Both these quaint objects are small, but later in the time of Charles II large stew-pans and saucepans of a more refined character came into use for serving food at table. It is not at all probable that the food was actually cooked in these saucepans, but that stews and similar foods, after being made ready, were poured in the silver vessels and kept hot until carried to the table where they could be put on a brazier or spirit lamp.

While earlier examples do exist, any that come on offer to-day are mostly of the late eighteenth and early nineteenth century and these are relatively plentiful. They are of various shapes with a turned wood handle and, as a general rule, a cover and applied lip.   Most of them are the bulbous shape (Fig. 69) similar to the iron saucepans which have known a revival since the introduction of the slow combustion cooking stoves.

Smaller ones, sometimes with a spirit stove, were used for preparing mulled wine, namely, wine heated and spiced.   These are sometimes called by the old name, pipkin, which was an earthenware cooking pot with a hollow earthenware handle that was either put in the hot ashes of the great open fireplace or set on a trivet.

TOBACCO AND SNUFF-BOXES

When a custom or habit becomes fashionable, it is condoned, otherwise it is condemned.   For example, snuff-taking to-day is regarded as a more or less unpleasant habit, but relatively few people disapprove of smoking; yet less than a hundred years ago, smoking was taboo while a snuff-box was something that every well-dressed gentleman carried.

Mrs. C. S. Peel gives us an interesting sidelight on the objection to smoking in *Early Victorian England* (Oxford University Press, 1934).   She tells us that, 'The ladies having retired, the gentlemen donned their smoking-caps and jackets or even complete suits . . . to prevent the dress coats and hair of the wearers from becoming tainted with the smell of smoke'.   Men were not allowed to smoke in the presence of ladies or in the street; before the introduction of rooms set aside for smoking, it was permitted in the garden, the stables, or the gun-room, and, after the servants had gone to bed, in the steward's room or servants' hall or 'in modest establishments, in the kitchen'.

There are varying accounts as to the introduction of tobacco to Europe, but it would seem to have been brought to Spain in about 1560 by Francisco Fernandes and about the same time to France by Jean Nicot, from whose name the word 'nicotine' derived. But while smoking soon became widely popular in Europe, it was virtually unknown in this country until Ralph Lane, the first Governor of Virginia, brought back pipes and tobacco when he returned in 1586, after which it became 'desired of all men'.

That last phrase is from a story which this writer heard when he was better acquainted with some of the Indian tribes of the South Western United States. According to this, an American Indian princess who lacked the personal qualities which attract the opposite sex prayed to her gods that the earth might open and swallow her and that she should rise again beautiful and desired by all men—the legend tells she rose again as the tobacco plant.

When silver boxes for tobacco were first used is open to question, but there is no doubt that they were in fairly general

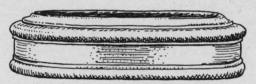

Fig. 70.   Tobacco-box with loose cover.   1709–10.   L. 4½ in.

use among the more wealthy men by the second half of the seventeenth century. They are almost invariably oval and quite plain except for an engraved coat of arms or similar insignia and perhaps some small ornamental band round the rim of the cover. As a general rule, tobacco-boxes have loose fit-on covers (Fig. 70) but with some examples the cover is hinged; similarly, while the average size is about 3½ to 4 inches long they were sometimes made rather larger and, as the engraved arms often denote, many of them once belonged to members of families who were prominent nearly two hundred and fifty or more years ago.

Snuffing or sneeshing, as it is called in Scotland, was a habit the Europeans copied from some of the native tribes in South America where it was first noticed by Ramon Pane on his second voyage with Columbus at the end of the fifteenth century. Less than a century later, it was popular in France where it was prescribed as a remedy for a nasal trouble which was prevalent at that time. Apparently the remedy became so popular that the 'patients' spread the virtues of *reniflement*.

It was indulged in to a certain extent in England during the seventeenth century, but at first it was not sold in the familiar powdered form but in what were called 'carottes' which were tightly rolled tobacco leaves. The 'carotte' was powdered by the snuff-taker on an iron rasp or rape rather like a small nutmeg grater which was mounted on carved ivory or wood, sometimes inlaid with mother of pearl.

In 1702, Sir George Brook's expedition to Vigo captured enormous quantities of grated snuff. After this had been sold and distributed in this country, snuff-taking soon became universally popular and within a short time small boxes of wood, horn, silver and even gold were as numerous as cigarette cases are to-day.

Gold and enamelled snuff-boxes inspired by the elaborate examples produced in France were made in England and Ireland, but here we are concerned more with the simple silver ones which were far more popular in this country.

Occasionally, you may come upon one fitted with a reading glass. These are oval in shape with the cover hinged at one end; at the other end a small magnifying glass is fitted to swing out from a recess in the box, the glass being in a shield-shaped frame so that when it is in the recess, the oval outline of the box is complete. Others are made with two compartments formed of two small boxes joined together each with a separate hinged cover. These were intended to hold two kinds of snuff and it might be suggested that one kind was reserved for the owner and his more intimate friends and the other for strangers to whom he might offer a polite 'pinch'. And some of the early nineteenth-century boxes of the larger size have a musical box in the base.

TUMBLERS

These amusing and entertaining cups (Fig. 71) are about 2 inches high and are made of heavy silver with a rounded bottom so hammered that the weight of metal in the bottom is proportionately greater than in the sides. This allows them to rock from side to side but prevents their overturning, even when filled with wine, in the same way that a weighted doll will roll from side to side yet 'remain on its feet' and, after a time, come back to an upright position.

They came into fashion during the time of Charles II at which time the silver goblets and other stemmed wine cups were no longer popular. Actually, the tumblers were a revival of a

FIG. 71.   Small bowl known as a tumbler cup.   1727–8.   H. 2¼ in.

similar little bowl-like cup probably made three centuries before, as there are references in quite early records to 'bolles' and 'boles of silver'.

VINAIGRETTES

These delicately made little boxes, while themselves relatively modern, can claim to be of ancient lineage for they are descended from the ancient pomander, a brief description of which will not be out of place here.

To the present time, it is a fairly common practice to push cloves into an orange for the purpose of inducing a pleasant perfume in a room—that, to all intents, is a repetition of the pomander. Cardinal Wolsey carried an orange 'whereof the mete . . . was taken out and fylled up agayn with the part of a sponge wherein was vyneger and other confecsions agaynst the pestylente ayers; to the whiche he most commonly smelt into . . . when he was pestered with many sewters' (suitors).

'Pomander' is a corruption of the early French *pomme d'ambre* (apple of amber) the amber being the wax-like substance, known as ambergris, from the sperm whale which gives off a pleasant perfume when warmed. A ball perfumed with ambergris, musk or other scent in a silver pierced frame was carried by a chain round the neck in medieval and later times as a protection against fevers or plague and also as an antidote to the unpleasant smells which prevailed in the streets in olden days.

Some of them were made with as many as eight compartments or loculi, to use the technical name, each of which was shaped like the segment of an orange so that when closed they formed a globular shape. The compartments had separate sliding lids and were for holding various pleasant smelling herbs, etc., such as rue, rosemary, lavender and others.

These interesting forerunners of the vinaigrette are well worth

FIG. 72. Vinaigrette. *Circa* 1800. L. 1½ in.

having, though specimens are by no means plentiful nor are they cheap; but as with all silverwork, especially small forgotten pieces, one does turn up occasionally in some unexpected place, unrecognized for what it is.

One early form of the vinaigrette was a small silver box with a pierced top fitted to the top of a walking stick. These date from the seventeenth century and there are other small ones which were made in the time of Queen Anne—but this does not suggest it is possible to obtain a specimen of either.

Any obtainable to-day were made in the last part of the eighteenth century or later. These are usually rectangular, engraved on the outside, with a finely pierced inner lid to the compartment which held the piece of sponge (Fig. 72). Some have a ring attached to allow them to be worn on a chain and others are without the ring and were carried in the handbag. They are of little use at the present time, except as interesting specimens of later small silverwork and pierced designs, though we have seen them used for postage stamps.

CHAPTER TWENTY-THREE

SCOTTISH SILVER

As THEIR NATIVE music is the sounding board of the temperament of a people, so those things they use in their homes chronicle their manners and way of life. If, for instance, the early silver of England is compared with that of Scotland, it is clear that while the former leaves no doubt as to the sumptuous manner of living the latter reflects an almost austere simplicity.

There is a general tendency to link Scottish silver with that made in England, but until the union of the two countries in 1707, the designs of the former were unaffected by those which were popular in England. And while during the eighteenth century ornamentation was used more freely in Scotland, it is evident from the examples that have survived that the traditional simplicity was preferred.

Any Scottish silver dating from the seventeenth century is rare indeed, for at no time did the lairds and chieftains of the north indulge in the extravagance known in the days of the English Stuart kings; even if their principles would have permitted this, their lack of material resources would have prevented it. And this explains why so few silversmiths were working in Scotland compared with the number in England and also why examples bearing the three towered castle mark of Edinburgh or the tree, fish and bell mark of Glasgow are far less plentiful than those punched with the mark of London or one of the English provincial assay offices.

While most of the silversmiths established themselves in Edinburgh or Glasgow or one of the smaller provincial centres, there is evidence that some of them, either from necessity or choice, travelled from place to place. Living like gipsies, these wandering craftsmen earned a precarious living by making spoons, ladles and other small pieces from silver which was supplied to them by the customer in the form of coins or perhaps some piece of worn silver.

Obviously this offered the 'gipsy' silversmiths an opportunity to increase their profit, which none of them had any objection to doing. When melting the silver handed to them, it was an easy matter to appropriate a small part and replace it by additional alloy. In this way, they were able to make silverwork at a price less than that charged by the established workmen and also, when handed coins, to keep these and draw upon the silver they had 'acquired' from other jobs.

These often skilled men continued to rove until at least the early part of the last century and Jackson refers to a family named Stewart of which succeeding generations travelled the north of Scotland as 'gipsy' silversmiths for over two hundred years. And it has been possible to trace the wanderings of some of the later members of the family by the various town marks which accompany the mark of one of these wanderers on different examples of their work.

Thus, Alexander Stewart was in Inverness in about 1770 and there made some silver which was marked by the local deacon with the town mark INS; another piece was marked at Tain some years later, at which time Alexander, Junr.—presumably a son— was visiting the district round Inverness where he made a few spoons; and work bearing the marks of the two mentioned and other members of the Stewart family has been found with the town marks of Dundee, Elgin and Wick.

Several shapes which were adopted by the Scottish silversmiths are not found in England and even where a similar shape was used, there are often noticeable differences by which the work of the two countries may be distinguished one from the other. These differences occur more particularly with Scottish silverwork of the earlier part of the eighteenth century as, for example, in the splendid globular-shaped tea-pots.

One of these tea-pots is illustrated in Fig. 73 and if this is compared with the English example shown in Fig. 8 several differences can be noted: The English pot has a flattish shoulder and a flat lid with a flush (concealed) hinge while the body tapers slightly toward the bottom which is wide and flat and 'sits in' a moulded foot; but the Scottish pot has a domical lid which

FIG. 73.   Scottish globular tea-pot with
tubular spout.   Edinburgh, 1726-7.   H. 6 in.

continues the curve of the body and forms a complete globe, because, instead of tapering downward, the circle is unbroken and rests on a short stem with a spreading foot.   Two other variations are the silver recurving scroll handle with the Scottish tea-pot and the applied hinge, though, as a rule, the latter is of the flush type shown in Fig. 8.

Though they are few, tea services with one of these Scottish tea-pots are known.   One made by William Aytoun bearing the Edinburgh hall-marks for 1733-4 was sold at Christie's a few years ago.   The tea-pot was accompanied by a small tray or stand with a simple reeded and escalloped border, a small sugar-bowl to match and a helmet-shaped cream-jug which was equally plain.   We refer to it here as a further instance illustrating the differences between the Scottish and English designs of this time—not with a view to inspire anyone with an urge to seek such a service, the value of which would prove beyond the elasticity of the average bank account.   Incidentally, with some of these services the cream-jug has a globular body similar to, but smaller than, the tea-pot.

Two other articles which were in common use in Scotland, the quaich and the small bell-shaped mugs, have no counterparts

among English silverwork.   The quaich or quaigh, as it is also
spelled, was the traditional Highland drinking cup and represented
to the Scots what the loving-cup was to the English, though it
does not seem to have become popular in the south of Scotland
until the end of the seventeenth century.

In quite early times, they were turned from a solid piece of

FIG. 74.   Scottish quaich engraved with intersecting lines, etc. 1736–7.   D. of bowl 6½ in.

wood in the same way as the mazers, and later made of staves of
wood bound with iron or silver, according to the financial
resources of the owner.   The one illustrated in Fig. 74 was made
at Edinburgh in 1736–7 and it will be noted that it is engraved
on the outside with a series of lines radiating from the bottom—
it is similarly engraved on the inside though this is not shown in
the illustration.   These lines are a relic of the early wooden
quaich and represent the shapes of the wooden staves; they are
intersected by three others running horizontally round the bowl
(suggesting the metal bands) and so forming a series of panels
with a single or double rose in some of the upper ones and a
feathered ornament in some of those below.   This style of
ornamentation is commonly found on the larger silver quaichs
such as would be made by the Edinburgh and Glasgow silversmiths.

Most of the smaller ones, which ranged from about 2½ inches
to 4 inches in diameter, were the work of men in the provincial
towns and these are often quite light, weighing less than 2 oz.
Some of the provincial quaichs of the eighteenth century are
what is called 'built-wood', that is made of the staves with silver
bands or hoops and a print in the bottom of the bowl, similar to

the print in a mazer described in Chapter Five; and like that of
the mazer, the print in the quaich is invariably decorated with
some engraved design, one of the favourites being a thistle
with a crown above and a motto, such as *Floreat*; occasionally,
a silver coin was inset in the bottom of the bowl to form a
print.

There is another small vessel, known in Scotland as a luggie,

FIG. 75. Scottish plain mug. H. 3 in.

which was also made of silver. These have only one handle
which should help even us 'Sassenachs' to recognize a luggie
when we see one, as a quaich always has two handles.

But no small piece of Scottish silver is more attractive than the
little mugs such as the one illustrated in Fig. 75. This type is
peculiar to Scotland and unlike any English mug—even though
the shape bears a likeness to some of the tea-cups which are still
made by the modern potters. These mugs are invariably bell-
shaped and though the one shown here is plain apart from a
moulded band round the body, many of them are decorated at
the bottom with a series of vertical lobes which have some
semblance to leaves.

Speaking of Scottish drinking vessels recalls a leather jack made
by Patrick Robertson of Edinburgh in 1764-5. This came to
the writer's notice some few years ago and is interesting as showing that Scotsmen were still 'drinking out of their boots', as a
Frenchman described it, for some years after the English had
discontinued using leather for drinking vessels.

This lone Scottish leather jack is only 7 inches high and therefore a puny thing compared with the English seventeenth-
century black-jacks some of which were more than twice that

height. They were of leather which had been waxed and blackened and were not unlike the leg of a man's riding boot with a handle and a silver band round the rim; we cannot therefore blame the French visitor who seeing men drink from these jacks told his compatriots that 'the English are an uncivilized race, they drink out of their boots'.

Examples still exist and it is probable that the relics of some of the larger ones moulder in the cellars of old inns. The very large jacks were used for carrying ale and other liquor from the cellar and the smaller ones which, as a rule, but not always, have a

FIG. 76. Caster decorated with cut-card work. Marked Edinburgh, 1703–4. H. 8 in.

silver lip-band were drinking pots. The latter vary in size and similarly in capacity which ranges from well over a gallon down to a quart.

Apart from the variations mentioned above and a certain few others of no importance, Scottish silver of the eighteenth century followed the same path as that of England, though at no time did Scotland accept the extravagances of the rococo period. Not that they refused to accept any of the ornamental forms which were introduced to England by the Huguenot silversmiths, but when any 'Frenchy' decoration was used, it was always of the most restrained type such as the beautiful cut-card work on the caster made by James Sympsone of Edinburgh in Fig. 76.

As the century advanced the English fashions came to be accepted and copied and, by the beginning of the nineteenth century, silver made in Edinburgh or Glasgow differs in no way from that of London or Birmingham—the precision of the machine makes all things akin.

CHAPTER TWENTY-FOUR

IRISH SILVER

ONE WITTY IRISH collector friend of ours, speaking of the repeal of the External Relations Act, said, 'Well it may persuade the English to acknowledge silver was made by Irishmen'. There is more truth than poetry in that remark for it is a common practice to use the all-embracing term 'English' when referring to the silverwork of the British Isles, thus ignoring both the Irish and the Scottish.

Actually, Ireland was producing magnificent work as early as the tenth century—at which time England was still in a relatively primitive state. And in recent years, a number of ancient Irish pieces have been brought to light in unexpected places. One of these important finds is the Ardagh chalice which with a small cup and four brooches was unearthed by a young man when he was digging potatoes near Ardagh in Limerick.

When Irish and English silverwork of any period is compared, it becomes clear that the former has certain well defined characteristics, particularly in the decorative treatment, which are peculiar to Ireland. Admittedly, some of the basic shapes of the later articles are similar, but, while the ornamental forms adopted by the English silversmiths were largely derived from the Continental countries and are conventionalized, the Irish give expression to that romance and fantasy which is inherent in these lovable and delightfully inconsequent people.

In the decoration, it is often possible to see something of that quaint whimsicality, that love of nature and that affection for the 'little folk' rather than the more stilted and symmetrical forms borrowed from the Continent. But it is not suggested that the Irish silversmith always introduced his native ideas, because when producing some important object, to the order of one of the prominent families, he followed the prevailing English fashion, as for example in the double-lipped sauce-boat in Fig. 77.

Ornamentation of the kind which is characteristically Irish is

FIG. 77. Irish double-lipped
sauce-boat. 1732–3. L. 6¾ in.

FIG. 78. Irish pierced and chased butter
dish and cover. 1742–3. L. 7 in.

perhaps more especially pronounced with cream-jugs, sugar-
bowls, butter-dishes and the dish-rings. While he accepted the
rococo forms, the Irish silversmith generally adapted them to his
own design and as of supplementary rather than primary importance—though it must be admitted that some of the Irish interpretations of the rococo result in a somewhat confused mixture.
And it is not uncommon to find silverwork chased with scrolls,
shellwork and similar elements combined with flowers, foliage
and pastoral scenes.

One favourite and attractive style of Irish work was achieved
by embossed and chased designs with the background cut away.

This is illustrated by the butter-dish shown in Fig. 78 the sides of which are chased with a design which includes flowers, trees, a milkmaid in an elaborate costume milking a rather crudely shaped cow with exceptionally long horns, a windmill, a swan and other objects of a pastoral character. The dish is fitted with a blue glass liner and the cover is similarly chased and pierced and has a cow as a handle. The finest examples of this form of decoration, however, are among the dish-rings which will be touched upon later in this chapter.

Even where the rococo scrolls and shell work are more predominant, scenes or some natural creatures would be introduced as is the case with the milk-jug in Fig. 79. The shape of this is very largely peculiar to Ireland and while the chased work round the upper part, above the moulded band, is essentially in the rococo style, the lower part is chased with large birds, probably intended for geese, standing in water. In other instances, little figures were combined with the scrolls and shell work. And sauce-boats on three legs also show the Irish love of nature's creatures, for they would copy the English shape with the long lip and wavy edge and use a fine scroll handle and legs with shell feet and a bold lion mask above, then decorate each side of the bowl with some rural scene such as a milkmaid milking a cow and a little farmstead and quaint trees in the background framed by quite elaborate rococo foliated scrolls.

Occasionally, the silversmith was content to omit his own ideas and to interpret the rococo style without variations and additions. An instance of this is illustrated in the sugar-bowl (Fig. 80) which is chased with scrolls fringed with rock-work and small flowers. At times, he would combine something of the rococo with something of the classic and add his own 'scenery'. For example, we have seen the helmet-shaped jugs (Fig. 79) with typical rococo feet, chased with classic festoons below and a farmyard scene complete with cows, trees and buildings above the moulded band.

Though Ireland was unaffected by the change in the standard of silver which resulted in the plainer styles in England during the early eighteenth century, the fashion crossed to Dublin and some

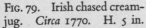

FIG. 79. Irish chased cream-jug. *Circa* 1770. H. 5 in.

FIG. 80. Irish chased sugar bowl. *Circa* 1770. H. 3 in.

beautiful pieces entirely free of ornament were produced by the Irish silversmiths of that time. Three such pieces are illustrated here: the caster (Fig. 81) which is one of a set of three has the octagonal pyriform shape, or, in simpler language, pear-shape with eight sides, a shape which is less severe than the quite plain pear outline, because the angles introduce light and shade, and the angles are continued up with the high cover which is pierced with small scroll and other forms.

There is a like simple beauty in the hexagonal chocolate-pot (Fig. 82) which also shows the skilful use of mouldings on the lid, round the body, the base and at the joint of the spout. These are mentioned separately because they are worth studying to appreciate fully their value as a distinctive ornamentation. It will be noticed that the pot has a small cover hinged to the larger cover which, in turn, is hinged to the handle socket. The purpose of the smaller one is to close the hole for the stick with which the chocolate was stirred, as explained in a previous chapter. And that the devotees of this pleasant drink insisted upon its being hot is evident not only in the spirit lamp but in the tiny hinged cover to the spout.

Monteith bowls copied from the English models were made in Ireland, but there was a general preference for the plain punch-bowls of which one is shown in Fig. 83. To anyone with a practical experience of silverwork who has 'hammered a few spots' these bowls are an outstanding tribute to the skill of the

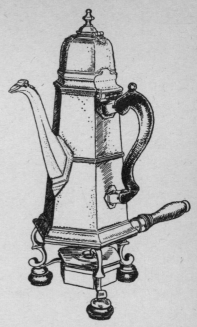

FIG. 81. Octagonal pyriform caster, Dublin, 1709–10. H. 7 in.

FIG. 82. Hexagonal chocolate-pot with stand and lamp on wood feet. Dublin, 1708–9. H. 14½ in.

makers, because they were raised, as it is called, from a flat circle of sheet silver by patient hammerwork.

We are tempted to describe the process, but that would lead us into the field of technicalities which have no place in this book. So we will be content with saying that the raising of such a bowl or any large silver object demands a mathematical precision in the use of the hammer and an almost tireless patience. Any attempt to 'hurry up' the work is very apt to be disastrous—Longfellow's lines 'The heights by great men reached and kept were not attained by sudden flight' could be applied to raising a fine piece of silver.

Certain shapes found with Irish silver work show a distinct Oriental influence as for instance the fluted dish (Fig. 84) which may well have been a design copied from the fluted work found among Chinese jade and porcelain.

FIG. 83. Plain punch-bowl made by Thomas Bolton, Dublin, 1714–15. D. 9¾ in.

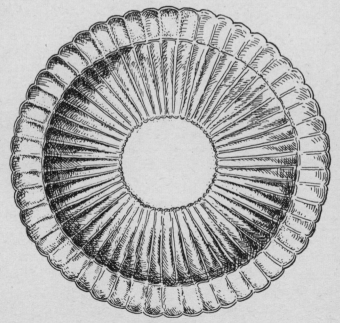

FIG. 84. Fluted fruit-dish. Dublin, 1723–4. D. 10 in.

DISH-RINGS

No silver article is more generally misunderstood than these really beautiful Irish rings—in England commonly, but quite wrongly, called 'potato rings'. As an instance of how little is known about them in England, we may quote one professed authority who concealed his ignorance of their intended use by suggesting that 'the actual purpose for which these rings were used is now forgotten'—a somewhat startling explanation considering that they first became popular in Ireland in about 1750 and were still fashionable to some extent in the early part of the nineteenth century.

Actually one of the rings was placed on the dinner table and served as an ornamental support or stand for, in this order, the soup-bowl, the oak potato-bowl (see Fig. 85), the dessert-bowl and lastly for the convivial punch-bowl, the intention doubtless being to protect the surface of the table from the heat. Some question has been raised as to whether the ring was used except for the potato-bowl, but various enquiries we have made at different times seem to support the suggestion that it was also used for the others.

There are three styles of these rings, each of which represents a distinct period. Those of the first period are quite shallow and the diameter of the rim is usually the same as that of the base. The spool-shaped sides at this time were ornamented with chased scrolls and flowers with the background cut away and the plain rim and base bands are unusually deep.

With the rings of the second period, which are higher, the Irish silversmith, taking advantage of the larger surface, gave full rein to his love of fantasy and the interweaving of rural scenes with the ornamental design. The one illustrated in Fig. 85 concedes something to the prevailing rococo style in the large foliated C-scrolls, but to the maker of that ring these were merely to 'fill in' the spaces between the farm buildings, the haystacks, the rooster and his wife, the cow and other details of the 'picture'.

Another may give his interpretation of an Oriental scene with

FIG. 85.   Dish-ring marked Dublin, 1760–1, and
oak bowl.   Ring 4 in. high; bowl 13 in. diam.

quaintly pictured Chinese architecture and amusing figures wear-
ing pancake hats; and with these he would combine huntsmen in
European costume carrying old-fashioned fowling pieces and
dogs running among the undergrowth.   Where he produced .
such scenes, he would add birds in flight or roosting on the tree
branches and both the birds and the trees are usually quite out of
proportion to the other objects; or the sides would be divided
into panels by scrolls, each pair of which were joined by a
medallion enclosing a formal leaf.

Each of the panels would perhaps picture some rural occupation
as one we remember which showed a fashionably gowned lady
gathering fruit and a farmhouse in the background.   That there
was an entire absence of any perspective caused no distress to the
silversmith who chased the design, nor did it worry him that the
lady's hat was hanging to her head 'by a hair' or that the fruit on

the tree was suspended from nothingness; but such little failings are noticed only when you look for them and, even when you see them, they add to the attraction of the dish-rings as they do to other similar Irish pierced work.

Those of the later part of the middle period generally show a free use of flying birds as part of ornamentation, or floral festoons with birds and squirrels or foliated scrolls with birds and fruit but attractive as these are, they lack something of the simple charm of the quaint pastoral subjects.

The rings of the third period are strongly influenced by the classic designs introduced by Robert Adam and are pierced with vertical slits with embossed medallions and festoons and similarly formal designs. This style undoubtedly enjoyed a certain vogue though it never superseded the earlier designs which continued to be made until the dish-rings went out of fashion.

SECTION 5
How the Faker Plays and Loses

CHAPTER TWENTY-FIVE

HIS SCHEMES AND HIS NEMESIS

SO LONG AS there are those who will 'take a chance', there will be a chance to take—and *vice versa*. One of our natural impulses is to gain an advantage over another and—forgetting that it works both ways—our normal common sense is blunted and we lose sight of the fact that haphazard knowledge is a weak antagonist against guile and trickery.

That brief philosophical homily comes from having been privileged to know and observe many who are interested in things of bygone days and discussing their 'treasures' with them. Those discussions have unfortunately shown how often the desire to own a particular object has resulted in its being purchased without first consulting some experienced person and how often this has meant a keen and expensive disappointment. Such disappointments occur more frequently with the buying of 'old' furniture, china, glass and, let it be added, paintings, because the fraternity who 'offer the chances' are considerably more impudent in misrepresenting any of these than they dare to be with articles made of silver.

Most people who are interested in silver at all are well aware that there are such things as hall-marks even if they know nothing about them nor what they signify; and this in itself is some deterrent, though not a serious one, to the exploitation of ignorance by the unscrupulous. Though few people would regard counterfeiting a hall-mark as serious as counterfeiting a coin, in actual fact it is, and the Act of 1913 provides for fourteen years' penal servitude as a reward for anyone who forges any die that is or has been used by an assay office.

After some practice, most people could forge a signature on a cheque, but it takes courage to present it for payment. It is the same with faking silver. Any skilled silversmith can copy the shape of a piece made in the days of the Queen Anne, early Georgian or any other period, and as we shall see 'hall-mark' it by various means; but it is quite another matter to dispose of it in such a way that the forger remains safe. At some time or another that article will be seen and examined by shrewd and experienced eyes and then woe to the 'skilled' maker. The authorities will trace its journey backwards from the person who owns it and they will persist until they arrive at its birthplace when the man who 'fathered' it will be put where he cannot get into mischief.

It is quite a popular idea that faking silver became a favourite pastime after collecting began to be really fashionable about forty-odd years ago, when the competition for rare specimens among wealthy enthusiasts caused values to rise and the demand to exceed the supply. But it was a lucrative art before that time, not for the purpose, so much, of making new pieces old as to dodge the duty which was repealed in 1889–90. And we can here quote a famous case which was tried in 1880 and which will show the tenacity of the Goldsmiths' Company in tracing the origin of spurious silver wares.

In 1872 and 1873 a London silversmith sold a customer a fairly large amount of table ware—actually it was a service of 643 spoons, forks and knives. That customer must have been both ignorant and gullible, for each of this large number of pieces had a bust of Queen Anne or of Prince George of Denmark at the end of the stem; but they were marked with the figure of Britannia, the lion's head erased and the date letter for 1703, so the customer bought them and went away happy.

He remained happy in the possession of these remarkable 'treasures' for six years, then came an emissary of Nemesis in the form of a friend who had made some study of old silver and of hall-marks. Recognizing that every piece was a fake and being a real friend, he told the owner the truth and Nemesis herself (known more particularly as the Goldsmiths' Company) was notified and the fun started.

All the articles were examined and tested and found to be below the Britannia standard of silver. That in itself was naughty, but that they bore forged marks added greatly to the wickedness of someone whom the Goldsmiths' Company set about to find. The dealer who sold them saved himself from punishment by revealing the name of the man he bought them from. The latter proved to be a working silversmith in quite a small way. When he was taxed with it, he claimed they were part of some silver he had bought or exchanged in 1872 and handed the matter over to some solicitor. In any event, the solicitor later produced invoices covering about 600 pieces and cheques for payment for it that were endorsed and had been through a bank. So the little silversmith went free though as the report puts it 'The circumstances bore a very suspicious appearance. . . .'

Then the Goldsmiths' Company began proceedings against the man from whom the working silversmith had said he had bought the troublesome table tools and after the usual prolix legal arguments and a considerable outlay for fees, this 'master mind' was fined £6,430 (£10 for each spoon, fork and knife).

This was a particularly flagrant instance and is selected to show both how carefully the public are protected and the power which the Goldsmiths' Company wield to ensure that protection. Whether it be one or many pieces in question, they keep up the pursuit to the source of the supply until they find it.

We have said in Chapter One that the Britannia and lion's head erased marks (instituted with the raising of the standard of silver in 1697) are still used by the Goldsmiths' Company. And if an article is made of this slightly more costly silver it will be punched with these two symbols which are to all intents exactly the same as those found on all silverwork made from 1697 to 1719–20. And though the type of the date letter is entirely different from that of the high standard period, and the maker's mark is now the initials of his christian and surnames instead of the first two letters of his surname, the faker is able to 'adjust' these differences.

Having obtained a modern copy of some article made of the

high standard silver in the style of the early eighteenth century, which has been assayed and marked with the Britannia and lion's head erased, it is an easy matter to 'doctor' it in a way to suggest it was made nearly two hundred and fifty years ago. All he has to do is to carefully wear down on a mechanical buff or polisher both the date letter and the maker's mark until they are indecipherable and the Britannia and lion's head erased until they are only just clearly recognizable; and the unwary victim naturally concludes that they have been worn by the lusty servants who have cleaned them over the years.

Another method of 'ageing', even if the potential profits are somewhat less, is to obliterate the king's head from an article bearing the hall-marks of a year between 1784-5 to 1821-2— after that time, the uncrowned leopard's head and the new form of lion 'give the game away'. For example, a piece made in 1816-17 could be 'back-dated' forty years and be convincing to anyone who was not more than usually observant. The date letter for both 1816-17 and 1776-7 is the small roman letter, a, the leopard's head is crowned, the lion is full-faced for both years, moreover, the shapes of the punches are very similar. But an experienced man would 'spot' where the king's head had been; which is one more instance of the advisability of relying upon those who have learned the answers to the problems set by the faker.

Whether the penalty for obliterating and defacing marks in the way described is sufficiently severe is highly debatable. It is an easy method of 'raising the value' and the penalty which is £5 for each defacement would not seem an adequate deterrent. But where the punishment fits the crime, as in the case of counterfeiting the actual punches or in transposing marks, the bad boys are less likely to 'take a chance'. Each of these is a felony and was punishable by death until 1773 when it was changed to transportation for fourteen years; and as we have said, anyone convicted of either offence to-day is liable to fourteen years' penal servitude.

Among the photographs in the writer's files are several of attractive plain pieces which brought trouble to one man some few years ago. On the back of one photograph is the terse official notation: '[So-and-so.] Tried and sentenced [date]. Example purporting to be Queen Anne 1706–7. Maker's mark, William Fawdry. Marks forged; analysis shows alloy of composition different from that used at period indicated by marks. Metal of varying quality. Other forged articles. Refused to disclose source from which articles obtained. Search proceeding.' We have omitted the man's name and the date, hoping his rather lengthy 'holiday' gave him an opportunity to reflect and reform.

Now a word as to the forged marks on those articles: Quoting from notes we made at the time, the outline of the figure of Britannia was good enough to deceive many, but when examined closely, the die had been cut by a man who had no real knowledge of the minor details of the genuine marks and the same comment applies to the lion's head erased; the date letter being angular offered no great difficulty to the forger and his reproduction was 'commendable'.

Actual forging is far less prevalent than what is known as transposition, which is the legal term for cutting genuine marks from an early specimen which is damaged and of little value and 'marrying' them to a modern article made in the style contemporary with the marks. The marks are then let in the new article and soldered. To the uninitiated, the outline of the joins are invisible, but the let-in piece as a rule shows if breathed upon and if the article becomes oxidized the outline is clearly revealed.

Transposing marks in this way is by no means a recent 'invention' as is shown by an entry of January, 1730, which is quoted in *Memorials of the Goldsmiths' Company* by Sir Walter Prideaux: 'Mr. Wardens took into consideration how to remedy an antient evil practice amongst ill-disposed Goldsmiths, of cutting out the Company's marks from pieces of old plate and soldering the same into new pieces which have never been tried at the Hall. . . . Now . . . Mr. Wardens ordered that the officers in the Assay Office . . . do strike the marks on every piece of plate as farr distant from each other as the same conveniently may be struck, so that they may not be cut out together.'

Formerly the various symbols composing a set of hall-marks were punched separately and the order that they should be 'farr distant from each other' is shown in the irregular placing of the different punches on earlier silver-work; in more recent years a compound punch (one comprising all the marks used by an assay office), is commonly used, when the several symbols are in line fairly close together.

However skilfully the insertion of old marks is done, the fraud is certain to reveal itself at some time—one might apply, in reverse, the Biblical admonition, 'Men do not put new wine in old bottles'. And while it would be possible to quote others, two examples which offer less difficulty to the faker will suffice, namely articles such as bowls and dish-rings with which a set of marks, usually taken from the stem of a spoon, is inserted in the circular foot.

Another allied practice and one more difficult to detect is to 'adapt' the marks on the bottom of some damaged or unimportant article to the bottom of a larger modern piece made in the style contemporary with the marks. For instance, a skilful hammerman can 'adapt' a round salt-cellar which is marked on the bottom to the bottom of a coffee-pot, jug or similar article. But here again, the fraud is bound to be revealed when the piece is examined by an expert. The circle of silver bearing the marks is generally too thin to serve as the bottom of the object to which it is soldered and is actually an extra bottom.

When marks are punched on silver, they naturally leave a clearly discernible trace of the pressure on the other side of the metal. Therefore when the marks are impressed on the outside of the bottom of a coffee-pot or similar article, the general outline of each one can be seen on the inside. But when the extra bottom bearing the marks is soldered on, there is obviously no trace of the impressions on the inside of the pot.

That is one of the obstacles to success that the faker rarely heeds. It has been said that it is the small things which he overlooks that bring a criminal to the dock, and the same can be said of the man who tries to 'manufacture' antique silver. He will take infinite trouble to achieve what should be a perfect specimen, yet will overlook some quite minor but obvious clue to his misdeeds.

We have in mind a large jug which caused some laughter in the end. Doubt had been expressed as to its being genuine and it was examined. It was marked at the bottom and there were 'signs' of the impress of the punches on the inside (for once the faker had remembered this important 'addition'). But the bottom inside was slightly convex and as the underpart of the bottom was more convex, the question was disposed of by our old friend Euclid's 'which is absurd'—two convexes on opposite sides of the same surface are impossible.

Any silver that has undergone the 'ageing' process is almost invariably quite plain. Wise as a counterfeiter may be in the ways of the inexperienced, he is largely ignorant of the styles which distinguish the different periods; and even if the humble craftsman who is his source of supply is asked to produce an article of a more or less ornamental character, mistakes in the 'interpretation' are obvious to anyone who is familiar with the original forms. Often, too, the faker's lack of knowledge of his history of styles in silver work will reveal itself by the insertion of early eighteenth-century marks in articles that did not come into fashion until many years after those marks were used.

In addition to transposing, there is the other branch of the faker's art, namely transforming. The latter is a 'major operation' by which an article of no particular use and therefore not saleable is changed to one for which there is a demand; and, what is important, the change can be made without affecting the original marks.

This can be better illustrated by a few examples, each of which, it must be admitted, is a tribute to the men who accomplish the transformation: One of the ogee-shaped (the pear outline) sauce-pans can be changed to a two-handled cup, though it is most probable that the date of the marks will be later than the time such a cup was in general use; a spoon with a trifid end, hall-marked during the late seventeenth century, may have a badly damaged bowl, but it can undergo an operation and reappear as a fork which is even more 'valuable' than the spoon perfect; a goblet is quite useless at the present time, but the faker sees it as a pierced sugar-bowl with a blue glass liner; a small mug may have been in a family for generations and, though useless, reverenced for its sentimental associations, but the 'surgeon in silver' has no such reverence—he transforms it into a small jug; similarly by adding three legs and a handle to a pap boat he produces a little sauce-boat or cream-jug; a discarded snuffer-tray by the addition of two glass pots with silver tops becomes an attractive inkstand and so on.

Many conversions such as those mentioned above were made to the orders of former owners. These people are to be admired for their practicality, because often they were able to replace a 'cabinet' piece by a useful household article. No objection should be raised against such conversions for they please the owner and offend no one even though, strictly speaking, they are illegal. But it is a very different matter when they are made, as they often are by the faker, solely for the purpose of selling them to the unwary at prices far above their real value.

Detection of the various types of 'wrong 'uns' comes only from the familiarity and experience gained from handling and studying genuine examples; and until you have proven to yourself that you can confidently divide the sheep from the goats, be advised to rely entirely upon an experienced 'shepherd'.

Disposing of faked silver is largely similar to the 'ramp' at race meetings where some tout will offer you a 'gold' ring or one set with a 'diamond' because he has lost his money—it is done 'quite privately'. Obviously, the faker dare not risk his 'wares' coming to the notice of any established dealer or offer them in a reputable auction room.

St. Matthew cautioned, 'Use not vain repetitions as the heathens do', but the writer will risk being ranked with the heathens and repeat the words of the chief of a firm of London valuers who some years ago, speaking of the machinations of the silver forger, said, 'Fraudulent trading is all done privately and it would have a speedy end if buyers would deal only with firms whose names are a warranty or would insist upon having the silver examined by accepted experts before completing the purchase'. How sound that advice was and is.

SECTION 6

Old Patterns produced by Modern Craftsmen

CHAPTER TWENTY-SIX

HANDMADE SILVER

FASHIONS CHANGE AND novelties appear and are forgotten, but the designs of long ago persist. That is a slightly lyrical way of saying that the things we call antiques retain their universal attraction not because they are old, but because they have rhythmic form which is pleasing to the eye and that indefinable character which distinguishes all work produced by the hand of the craftsman from that of the machine.

To-day, we are so accustomed to the machine-made product, it might almost seem that handicraft was among the so-called lost arts; but what man has made in the past, man can make to-day and any silver article of whatever age can be reproduced in our own time; and when made by hand and close attention is given to the minor details, the modern copies lack nothing of the beauty of the original except that subtle colour tone which only Time can bestow.

To reproduce the old designs the silversmith not only has to be highly skilled, but equally he must have a personal liking for and a knowledge of the history of early silver work. Such men have gained their skill in the same way as those of long ago—namely, by serving an apprenticeship to a recognized master; and, while they are by no means numerous, it has seemed, in more recent times, that there is a growing tendency among young men to regard silversmithing as an art and to pass through the various stages from novice to master-craftsman, rather than become merely automatons attending a machine.

We used the term 'indefinable character' in connection with handmade silver work. While this cannot be described exactly, it can perhaps be explained, for it is the result of the thousands of hammer strokes necessary to shape or raise, as it is known technically, a flat sheet of metal to the desired form and the later planishing—planishing is hammering the surface with a small hammer to smooth out the marks of the larger hammer used in raising. But if you look closely at a hand-made silver article it is possible to see traces of tiny indentations which give an elusive light and shade. Another feature with hand-made silver is an attractive bluish-grey colour which is also a result of the hammering it has undergone.

These characteristics might be illustrated by the following incident: A lady who had received a cheque with which to buy herself a present asked the writer to take her to see some modern reproduction silver tea-pots. There were a large number to select from in the showroom to which we went. The lady who, incidentally, knew nothing about silver work, chose a copy of the Queen Anne pear-shaped type (see Fig. 7) and seemed quite content. Then, strolling around the showroom, she came to another group of tea-pots of exactly the same shape and size. Taking one down and looking at it, she said, 'I like this one better than the one I have chosen.' When it was pointed out to her that the price was higher than the one she had previously selected, she asked rather tartly why it should be, considering it was exactly the same. On being asked why, if it was exactly the same, she preferred it, her answer was she didn't know.

As we have said, her knowledge of silver was nil, but her preference was an expression of that unconscious admiration which even a novice has for the work of man's hand as distinct from that of the machine—the first tea-pot she selected was machine made, the second had been raised by hand from a circular sheet of silver. And, if at some time you are offered an opportunity to see the mechanical methods of producing silver articles or a craftsman diligently hammering up a shape, you are advised to take advantage of it.

By the mechanical processes the metal assumes its intended

form with uncanny speed; and you will find the movement of the craftsman's hammer almost mesmeric in its fascination. In fact, it is not unlikely that watching that same craftsman will inspire you with an ambition to try your hand at metal work. And as a relief from the daily round and a means to enjoy a sense of accomplishment, the writer knows no hobby more satisfying.

We illustrate with this chapter some present-day reproductions of seventeenth- and eighteenth-century originals. The standing-salt (Fig. 86) is a copy of that now rare type which was fashionable from the last few years of Elizabeth's reign to the time of Charles I. If this is compared with the sixteenth-century standing-salt illustrated in Fig. 1, it will be seen that it has a similar cylindrical shape, but is quite plain; the disappearance of the boldly embossed ornamentation signifying the effect of the Puritan influence which, as we have mentioned, began to show itself during the early Stuart period.

There is also a marked difference between the covers of the two salts. That in Fig. 1 fits closely over the salt-well and has the tall ornament surmounted by the figure of a bearded man holding a spear which is typical of the Elizabethan style; but the slightly later style shown in the copy (Fig. 86) has a sort of canopy in the form of an inverted bowl raised on scroll brackets fastened to the rim of the salt-well with a tall steeple-like finial which is similar to the finial of the steeple-cup in Fig. 2. An original 'steeple-salt' which was made in the reign of Charles I was among the Swaythling silver sold at Christie's in 1924 when it was bought by Crichton Bros. for £1,450.

The cylindrical caster (Fig. 87) is another example of the fine copies which modern silversmiths are making from old models. This was the first type of separate caster to be used in England and was introduced from France during the time of Charles II. Original sets of three, one large and two smaller, were made in the time of William and Mary and similar sets of the modern reproductions are obtainable, as they are made in sizes ranging from 7½ inches to 5½ inches high. And all the other styles of casters, both plain and octagonal, which were fashionable at different times during the eighteenth century and which have

FIG. 86. Modern copy of steeple standing salt. H. 15 in.

FIG. 87. Modern cylindrical caster with bayonet fastening copied from an early original.   H. 7 in.

FIG. 88.   Modern dredger or kitchen pepper copied from an early original.   H. 3 in.

FIG. 89.   Modern copy of the Treasury type inkstand.   L. 9 in.

been described in an earlier chapter are to-day copied from original models.

Whether a massive medieval standing-cup, a large racing trophy of Queen Anne's time or a set of the small, round salt-cellars of the early Georgian period, none offers any difficulty to those modern silversmiths who can express their skill through the medium of hand-tools.

Looking through the drawings of the examples of old silver which are illustrated in this book recalled those of reproductions which the writer has in his files; and comparing the old with the new shows how accurately the copies follow the originals. For example, the early Georgian globular tea-pot (Fig. 8) is a particularly popular model and the reproductions are exact in every detail even to the faceted spout, and the accompanying covered sugar-bowl and little cream-jug are equally faithful to the originals.

Similarly, there are several coffee-pots and chocolate-pots which repeat the size, shape and minor features of those made over two hundred years ago. One coffee-pot in the style of the early straight-sided example (Fig. 22) has the same ornamented spout showing the rococo influence, shaped handle and low moulded domical cover with a baluster finial. And a tall pot which might well have been copied from the one in Fig. 25 has exactly the same shaped body and high cover, the handle is at right angles with the spout, the thumb-piece is in the same position on the cover and even the tiny hinged flap on the spout.

Obviously, there are few of us who would not prefer the originals to the copies, however perfect the latter may be, but sometimes an original is beyond the reach of our bank balance. In such instances, we can always fall back on the present-day silversmith to satisfy our needs, if not our wants.

This suggestion is based upon personal experience. Over the years this writer was in charge of an important private collection of rare old silver. During that time, he was guilty of more than one breach of the tenth commandment, for it is not humanly possible to be constantly handling fine pieces without wishing to own them. For the time being, the coveter had to be content with photographs of the several desired objects and hope—hope, because there was always the possibility of a good reproduction of one or more of them becoming available.

Probably the most intense yearning was for a globular tea-pot which had been made in the shop of the celebrated Paul De Lamerie in the reign of George II. It was quite plain apart from some delicate engraving on the shoulder and lid and though, in view of the keen demand for De Lamerie silver, the value was far too high to be even considered, the possibility of finding a copy of a similar one remained. Some years later, that hope was realized when describing the tea-pot to a London dealer who mentioned a man who had once copied a tea-pot by De Lamerie. Actually it proved to be a reproduction of the one we were seeking and within an hour it had changed ownership.

In one or two other instances, working drawings were made from the photographs and we put on overalls and worked at the bench enjoying the hammering and seeing the metal take shape. It is not suggested, however, that those without practical experience should emulate this—because the results can be very disappointing unless you have learned how to handle the many kinds of hammers and other tools.

Though we are concerned more with early silver which can still be of everyday use, it may be of interest to refer briefly to the modern reproductions of one or two which were in use during the days of the Stuart kings, as some of these are quite suitable as a centre ornament on a table. For instance, a copy of one of the steeple-cups such as is illustrated in Fig. 2 is particularly effective on a medium sized table, for while they are upward of 18 inches high, the base is relatively small, so that it occupies little space; and this applies equally to one of the tall standing-salts, such as Figs. 1 and 86. Similarly, a copy of a Charles II two-handled cup and stand (see Fig. 4) on a larger table invariably introduces both a distinctive character and not a little romance to a modern setting.

It is sometimes thought that the copying of old models is a recent phase of silver work, but it is not so. As we have remarked before, many of the silversmiths of the early nineteenth century remained faithful to the traditional designs of the previous century. And after the public tired of the monstrosities which were introduced as 'New Art' during the Victorian period, there was a marked revival of interest in reproductions of eighteenth-century silver work. Catalogues of about a hundred years ago include what were called 'antique patterns', but while these were based upon earlier shapes, the silversmiths of that time were inclined to experiment with adaptations and introduce details foreign to the original model, whereas the craftsman of to-day will rarely attempt such 'improvements'.

Wealthy people of Victorian days were no more averse from display than those of any other period and in addition to articles for general use, such as tea services, coffee-pots, chocolate-pots, candelabra, candlesticks, inkstands, etc., the silversmiths produced large dinner services complete with various types of covered dishes, massive soup-tureens, punch-bowls, wine coolers, wine bottles and other objects of an ostentatious character copied from models which had been fashionable at different times during the eighteenth century.

We mentioned above the Victorian silversmith's tendency to depart from the original models in making his 'antique patterns'. This is shown in the several pieces of the tea service in Fig. 90 which was made about 1850. The basic shapes are those of the early Georgian style, but when each is analysed, certain adaptations are observable: The cream-jug has the plain pear-shaped body of the early eighteenth century (see Fig. 12), but the rim is the helmet-shape of the classic or Adam style (see Fig. 14); the same may be said of the bowl which instead of having the plain low moulded foot (see Fig. 15) is raised on a short stem and ornamental foot. Both the kettle and tea-pot reproduce the globular shape fairly faithfully, but the spout of each is far less graceful and the hinges of the lids more clumsy than those of the originals (see Fig. 8); again the tall stand with the kettle has disproportionate snake-like supports in place of the rhythmic scrolls such as are illustrated with the early Georgian kettles in Figs. 18 and 19.

Here a word regarding cleaning: It is not necessary to

FIG. 90.   Tea service of the so-called 'antique patterns' made in about 1850.

plaster periodically all the household silver with a coating of damp whitening or other powder and then laboriously brush and rub it off. Those articles which are in daily use on the table and which normally pass through the process of washing-up will retain their natural soft brilliance if they are washed in clean hot water with a soapy rag and, while still warm, dried with a dry soft tea-cloth; but let it be stressed that the water and soapy rag must be free from any grease and the tea-cloth dry—do not these same essentials apply to ensure that the glazed surfaces of china plates, dishes, cups and saucers are bright and without smears?

Silver that has become slightly oxidized—namely, has a dull brown film on the surface—can be easily restored by the use of an ordinary laundry soap and hot water. Where an article has perhaps been overlooked for some while and the discoloration is consequently more pronounced and difficult to remove, the writer has found the following effective: Put the silver object in a bowl of very hot water in which a handful of common washing soda has been dissolved; the silver should be completely covered by and left in the water for a short time. Then rub it with a recognized polishing powder—with emphasis on the 'rub', for no amount of powder is any use without at least a modicum of elbow grease; wash off the remains of the powder in hot water, wipe dry and finish by rubbing with a dry cloth.

Such articles as vases, candlesticks, knife handles and others which are made of thin silver filled with composition, or 'loaded' as it is called, should *not* be given the 'immersion treatment'.

It is very unwise to use a brush with a spiral wire handle to clean the inside of a silver vessel as the wire invariably rasps the edges of the rim; many a small article, a little pear-shaped cream-jug for instance, has suffered considerable damage in this way. Again, if a silver article should be bruised (dented) or damaged in any way—even slightly—it can always be repaired by a skilled man; and it is advisable that such repairs should be done at once, otherwise it is likely the article will be relegated to some cupboard and neglected.

BIBLIOGRAPHY

CRIPPS, W. J.: *Old English Plate.* 9th ed. 1906.

JACKSON, SIR C. J.: *An Illustrated History of English Plate.* 1911. 2 vols.

JONES, E. ALFRED: *Old Silver of Europe and America.* 1925.

OMAN, C. C.: *English Domestic Silver.* 1934.

PHILIPS, P. A. S.: *Paul De Lamerie; a Study of his Life and Work.* 1935.

WATTS, W. W.: *Old English Silver.* 1924.

WENHAM, EDWARD: *Domestic Silver of Great Britain and Ireland.* 1931.

Catalogues and Descriptive Books of Collections and Exhibitions

BURLINGTON FINE ARTS CLUB: *Exhibition of a Collection of Silver-smiths' Work of European Origin.* Illustrated catalogue. 1901.

CARRINGTON, J. B., and HUGHES, G. R.: *The Plate of the Worshipful Company of Goldsmiths.* 1926.

CRIPPS, W. J.: *College and Corporation Plate.* 1881.

ELLIS, H. D.: *A Short Description of the Ancient Silver Plate belonging to the Worshipful Company of Armourers and Brasiers.* 1892.

—— *A Supplemental Description* (to the foregoing). 1910.

FOSTER, J. E., and ATKINSON, T. D.: *An Illustrated Catalogue of the Loan Collection of Plate exhibited in the Fitzwilliam Museum (Cambridge), May, 1895.* 1896.

GARDNER, J. STARKIE: *Old Silverwork, chiefly English, from the XVth to the XVIIIth Centuries.* A catalogue of the loan collection exhibited at St. James's Court, London, in 1902. 1903.

JEWITT, L., and HOPE, W. H. ST. JOHN; *The Corporation Plate and Insignia of Offices of the Cities and Corporate Towns of England and Wales.* 1895. 2 vols.

JONES, E. ALFRED: *The Old Royal Plate in the Tower of London.* 1908.

—— *Illustrated Catalogue of the Collection of Old Plate of J. Pierpont Morgan, Esquire.* 1908.

—— *The Old English Plate of the Emperor of Russia.* 1909.

—— *The Old Plate of the Cambridge Colleges.* 1910.

—— *The Gold and Silver of Windsor Castle.* 1911.

MOFFAT, H. C.: *Old Oxford Plate.* 1906.

OXFORD: *Catalogue of a Loan Exhibition of Silver Plate belonging to the Colleges of the University of Oxford.* 1928.

SHAW, H. and MEYRICK, SIR S. R.: *Ancient Plate and Furniture from the Colleges of Oxford and the Ashmolean Museum.* 1837.

The history of the assay offices of England, Scotland and Ireland and tables of hall-marks and marks used by silversmiths are to be found in

CHAFFERS, W.: *Hall-marks on Gold and Silver Plate.* 9th ed. 1905.

CRIPPS, W. J.: *Old English Plate.* 9th ed. 1906.

JACKSON, SIR C. J.: *English Goldsmiths and their Marks.* 1905.

PRIDEAUX, SIR W. S.: *Memorials of the Goldsmiths' Company.* 1896–7. 2 vols.

INDEX